WELCOME RIVER

Sometimes a Fish out of Water Dances

The first thing that caught her eye was a shimmering fish handsomely flitting around in the water. As she approached, the fish paused and hovered above the water long enough to look her square in the eye. To her shock, he gargled the word, "Hello!" Before she could react, he was back in the water, then exuberantly jumped up again and, with a Latinesque roll of his words and a smile, said, "My name is Fredrico," then dove back into the water.

Not wanting to be rude, when he popped his head up again, Stella replied quite traditionally (despite this interaction being anything but traditional): "Good day. My name is Stella." He responded with a flip in the air and a splash, as if to celebrate the beginning of her journey.

Fredrico was brilliant red, flashy and expressive. His opalescent scales shimmered gold in the sunlight. The tips of his fins were trimmed in a fiery orange so vibrant it dared the water to extinguish it. As her eyes followed his lustrous fins moving flamboyantly, she was connecting the words *flamboyant* and *buoyant*—and the fact that this fish possessed *both* of these qualities so beautifully made her giggle to herself and think, "This fish is flamBUOYANT!"

"It's a pleasure to meet you, dear Stella," he said while bobbing gently in the water, "You have entered into a fantastical place, made

Spiraling Up

for you, by you! On Spiral-Up Mountain, you will create a path of the greatest good to find your inner light and your soul self."

Not having caught up to the moment at hand, she hesitantly replied, "I don't understand."

"Well," he started, "You probably know what it means to spiral down, like when you can't quite hang onto the status quo and keep feeling like you aren't getting anywhere." Stella did indeed understand that feeling. "Spiraling up is the opposite! You are here to rise up the mountain within, on a journey to learn about yourself, how to discern what feels right for you and how to live as you choose to be."

"Spiral-Up Mountain," he added, "is a place where you come face-to-face with the circle of life. While you're there, things flow by you, sometimes once, sometimes over and over…." He flipped about in the water to demonstrate. "You will discover how to choose what's on your path and how or if it returns. Learning how to do that is an important skill to ascend in life instead of heading down or round and round, never feeling like you are getting anywhere. Like the mountain itself, as you elevate, the path is consolidated with fewer delays in between shifting directions. It resembles the way your choices become clearer, your actions become more intentional and your self-awareness more refined. It simply keeps getting easier as you elevate."

"I can do that?" Stella asked. "You are already doing it," he replied. Then he told her to *say* it instead of ask it.

"I CAN do that!" she boldly exclaimed with a smile. "Wow, that felt good."

"That whoosh of good feeling is what it feels like when you are living your being," Fredrico continued. "It's a feeling that you are doing what you are meant to do and that your actions have meaning and value beyond yourself. You matter and what you do matters. You are creating the resonance of a life in tune, and when you make choices that align with who you are and what you choose to be, that tune becomes a symphony for the greater good of all. That's one of the keys!"

"Keys? Like the typewriter keys that unlocked the gate?" Her eyes glowed with excitement at this synchronicity but then became preoccupied with the next thought. "I don't know, Fredrico. It sounds like a lot of pressure. Who am I to resonate anything for the good of all? It all sounds nice but exhausting. Besides, I'm not sure I believe any of that." What she said felt heavy with sadness, and Fredrico watched her sit with this feeling before going on trying to convince him, and herself, that she wasn't worthy. "You may not know this, but that's not how the *real* world works. And I'm not a musician. How am I supposed to write a symphony?"

Shaking her head, Stella was feeling frustrated and blocked with disbelief. There were *far* too many things beyond her control that affected her every day. "It all sounds a bit fishy to me," she let out, suddenly laughing. Then, becoming aware that perhaps that was rude, but still enjoying it thoroughly, she said, "I'm sorry, I couldn't resist," to which he exclaimed, "You said that to a talking fish! Ha! That's *fin*-tastic!" They giggled together as Fredrico joyfully danced on the water.

This interaction lightened her mood.

He spoke again, "You have entered a new world, a fantastical world and it's full of adventure meant to guide you to what matters most…you. As you walk this journey, keep an open and curious heart, infused with the childlike wonder of the mind. Speak your questions. They will help you discern the source of many feelings. Even more importantly, listen for the answers." That advice landed with gravity.

Fredrico continued, "You will come across 5 keys, each one unlocking something within. The Map Key guides your compass, the Safe Key keeps you grounded, the Resonant Key harmonizes your tune, the Generator Key energizes your possibilities and the Answer Key will help you understand what you've always known. This land of suspended belief is as real as you allow it to be, and if you allow it to be, it will be real. That is how THIS world works."

He poured forth more droplets of wisdom: "Don't be frightened. Darkness that you fear within will dissipate in the light of your awareness. Trust that when you stumble, you will rise. You are safe in this land of infinite love. Allow for the full experience, especially the hard parts." And with a flick of his tail, he dove underwater and was gone.

"Hello? Goodbye? Fredrico?" She was suddenly alone and calling out to a fish. She was curious about how this would unfold, whatever it was. She felt okay about it, though, in a cautious, humble way. It was all very surreal, so naturally she was perplexed "Disbelief for sure. *Suspended belief?* Can I do that?" she asked herself, "Where am I anyway?" She looked around for some sort of path.

There was only brush.

"Of course I can do this!" she exclaimed loudly, surprising herself. This scenario reminded her of the Faerie tales of her childhood, the ones her Grandma would read to her that taught her virtues like ethics, bravery, kindness and chivalry using a cast of talking critters in magical settings. If this really was the beginning of her own Faerie tale, it would make her both the main character of the story *and* its author.

The thought of this possibility made her heart happy. It seemed so precious to feel this way, a way she had not felt for a long time. Stella responded to this inner glow with a declaration: "If this is the story of me, then I allow myself to experience it fully with suspended belief. I am grateful to learn all I can. I will walk with an open heart and a curious mind. I will listen to the fish!" She chuckled to herself.

Welcome River

There was no longer any reason for her to stand there, so she took a deep breath, releasing trepidation, and began to follow the river's edge. In no time at all, it became a small walking trail.

Fredrico

CONFLUENCE CLIFFS

Where Fear Meets Trust

The oddity of moments earlier lingered in her mind. She was on firm ground, but she felt an overwhelming sense of instability creep in. Being guided by the tree line, she just kept walking, still in awe, trying not to let her mind spiral down.

No more than a few feet in front of her was visible because of the rolling haze, though she knew she was at the river's edge beyond the brush wall. On the other side of the trail, she caught a glimpse of miniature trees through the low brush, smaller than she'd ever seen. She stopped immediately and leaned over, expecting to see a tiny village of ladybugs or some other delightful magical microcosm. Instead, she promptly recoiled and gasped!

Pulling herself back in elastic-like retreat from the space, she vacated the place held a split second ago. Falling backwards, she landed hard with a jarring knock to her senses that required sitting quite a few moments to catch her breath before she could even think about what she had just seen.

Forgetting all about the path ahead, she curiously crawled toward the mysterious edge of the walkway while keeping low to the ground to ensure she would not topple over. What she saw chilled her. She realized she was on a vast cliff, with a sheer-faced wall jagged enough to climb, or descend to a bottom she could not see.

She lay on her belly with barely her eyes and her fingertips hanging over—heights were never much her thing. She thought it wasn't supposed to be this way, fearful and dangerous. Perhaps it wasn't.

Her reaction was based on her experiences from another place and time, not now. In this moment, it almost felt like someone had left the curtain of fog pulled back too far and she was looking behind the scenes at a journey that wasn't hers. That thought came wrapped in comfort and gratitude.

Easing back on the fear, she relaxed and allowed her eyes to focus on the miniature forests she perceived. She realized that if they were visible from her height, it was only because of their massive size. They most certainly were not tiny. Perforated between the trees she could see what appeared to be another trail, or perhaps the same one at a much lower place down the mountain.

With no interest in wandering down that path, she gathered her senses and pulled herself back onto her feet. As soon as she stood up, the internal dialogue started; she had blindly walked unaware that a single misstep could have ended it all. The *what ifs*, *could haves*, *should haves* and *never agains* flooded her mind as she scolded her lack of... well, everything!

"What is this fool's errand I'm on? Am I too careless? Am I ready for this? Who am I kidding?!" she exclaimed out loud, from a place of feeling like a fraud. She believed that if she didn't die on this journey, she'd be discovered for her foolish self and be alone.

Stella ultimately trusted she had what it took to make her own way, yet she often let self-doubt stop her from moving forward. Not one to give up, though, she got up and continued walking the trail.

"AND," she said sternly, correcting herself, "I AM on this journey. I did not fall to my end. I reacted quickly to a perceived risk and adjusted myself to stay present. I can keep myself safe even if I don't know all the dangers around me. Alright," she continued to speak to herself, "That's the focus I want. The wins. Don't focus on the *maybes* and the *might haves* when they don't exist." With that thought, she created a bridge to an evolution that started long before she arrived at Spiral-Up Mountain, a testament to all she had done, and it felt good.

Taking her own words to heart, she stood tall and began again to walk ahead.

THE MAP KEY

*Remove Barriers to Create
Open Space Within*

CLEARING

STICKY CREEK

Pushing Through the Bog of a Life in Progress

A gentle bend turned into the woods, and suddenly the trail was gone. Unsure if what appeared to be was not, Stella felt lost, and without any bearings, she wandered aimlessly through the forest. She started to think she might have been seeing the same trees over and over. "Am I going in circles?" she asked no one, but someone spoke.

A heady voice carried a heartbeat within a word.
Forward
She walked. Overwhelmed, she picked up her pace.
Momentum
Stella ran, then fell into a bog.
Misstep
She struggled to move.
Sinking
The words came faster as she struggled.
Screaming
Fighting
Crying
Then they slowed.
Resting

Breathing

Thinking

Planning

Doing

Failing

Redoing

Conceding

She trudged through as best she could.

Exhaustion

Then she sank further.

Calamity

Inspiration

She reached for a nearby branch broken from a tree.

Motivation

Action

She pulled herself to solid ground.

Freedom

Exhalation

Gratitude

Humility

Serenity

Stella greeted the voiceover guiding her steps.

Acknowledgement

Connection

Then she listened.

Expression

Direction

Progression

Momentum

Resilience

Reflection

Standing, she felt ready to move forward.

Acceptance

Expansion

She allowed the words to saturate her mind.

Fulfilling

Aligning

Evolving

Enlightening

She took her next step towards her path.

Destiny

The words rang through her with intense singularity, somehow capturing each moment with clarity as if calibrating her intentions, her actions and her feelings with divine accuracy. She no longer felt disoriented, despite having no idea where she was and being caked by the murkiness of a dank forest pocket.

In the silence, between breaths, the softly stern voice spoke again:

At any step of a journey,
Fear can flood in.
Trauma and worry,
Grief and shame
Tear us from within.
There is a way of lightness
That will carry you in ease.
Your path will help you find it.
Release your fears and breathe.
A map within is the key
To your history in tow.
Let your heart be the compass

Spiraling Up

> *And your truth it will show.*
> *Trust in your worth and believe in the possibilities.*

And then the voice was gone. Propelled forward while absorbed in the words, she was now standing at the edge of the sun's touch, with a beautiful field of wildflowers in view. The sun danced in the breeze across the skyline, highlighting a million petals with a waxy glow. Smiling, she thought the whole scene reminded her of a big box of crayons.

Internally, she was hollering, "Who starts a journey like this? What is going on around here?" Her mind was rolling like the rapids.

Stella was a clever gal, a woman of wit and wisdom. She knew, she believed, and had to believe, she could find her way through. She knew she had to realign her thoughts to even begin to conceive of this, so she tried to mentally release the chaos and breathe. Repeating the words she had just heard, *"Let your heart be the compass,"* she imagined what doing this would feel like and where her compass would point her now.

She listened for the guidance of her heart, and with a slow, focused breath, she let her it guide her. "I am ready," she boldly declared, and with that, she stepped into the warmth of the sun again.

FLUTTER FIELD
Jump Ahead to Fall Back

Not long after departing the forest, Stella approached a field that had no visible end. It was splattered with color as if by a paint brush that had been flicked across a page. Wildflowers and grass swayed like ocean waves as the wind swept its breath across their tops.

A simple trail was worn with travel just enough to show her it was there. Taking an inhale ripe with floral scents under a blue sky, she skipped along until she found a comfortable easy stride. As she walked, she was getting bugged. Nearly silent and annoying flicks of motion were spiraling around her, one moment flying past her eyes and the next skimming the hairs on the back of her neck. She didn't like it.

Little irritants gradually got bigger with each step. They were no longer tiny gnats. Mosquitos and crickets, ladybugs and moths were suddenly invading her space, buzzing, tapping, hovering and intent on tormenting her. All the flies—butter, dragon, house and everything winged in between—seemed quite terrifying in those numbers, and she saw no escape as she progressed through her present environment.

In an outburst of fear and disgust, she quickly reacted with little thought and began running fiercely, waving her hands, screaming, "Go away!" She kept running until nearly out of breath. It was then that she felt a sharp piercing stab in her hand. In a singular motion, she grasped her hand, stopped her running, collapsed her legs and fell onto her back in exhaustion and pain on the path.

As she lay there holding her hand close for comfort, she regained her senses and began to settle into the horizontal plane she found herself in. "Breathe in, breathe out," was all she kept repeating to herself. When at last she examined her hand, she saw she hadn't been stung after all.

The sky was barely visible through the dense collection of flying critters, though they seemed to stay along the flower tops going about their busy, buzzing lives. As her eyes settled down further, she noticed the thorns. Gnarly spikes protruded from vines cleverly wrapped around the stems of dancing flowers that she would have admired from a loftier point of view.

It was clearly a thorn that stabbed her hand, as it was still in there. She yanked it out with a realization that rippled to the next aha moment: she was the reason she was "stung"—she freaked out! All that flailing about caused her to close her eyes to what was really in front of her. It disabled her from being able to think in the moment, therefore she was unable to proceed with care for herself in the process.

It was in moments like these she remembered her old life, how familiar this feeling of reaction and mindless survival felt, how she hoped to never feel it again. She knew she had to make the choice to learn to be present and thoughtful in any given moment if she was to truly depend on herself.

She continued to lie on this quiet path a few more moments, observing the rest of her surroundings. She noticed the vines clinging for support to the flowers, prompting her to think of some of her old relationships. They too had weak roots that barely held below the surface, causing the person to cling to her for support. Unlike the flower, whose roots grow deep and stand tall on their own, the vine survived by attaching itself tightly with no regard for the fact that it might result in the flower's demise.

This is a wild place, she thought. She was surprised at how a vine could bring her to relationship clarity. She observed the stems that encountered the resistance of the thorny vines had more substantial stems and broader leaves than those that didn't. It was *because* of the burdening vine that the flowers learned to grow strong and bloom upright as they were destined to do. She just needed a change of perspective to see that both the flower and the vine served a greater purpose and helped each other to grow.

Just then, the sun began to cast its rays upon her as if to kiss her forehead and say, "It's time to rise and begin again." Slowly she stretched herself upwards, acknowledging her role in creating this moment and giving grace to all of the living things in the field. She then turned with her back to the sun and began to walk again.

From the winged creatures to her beating heart, all was aflutter through this place, so she called it Flutter Field. She stood as high as the flowers as she took one step after the other, this time with an inner calm and presence. The feeling of uneasiness she'd been carrying for months was replaced with a quiet introspection of what she would rather carry, and that alone was a weight lifted. She felt good.

There was no disturbance from those that fly; they simply went about their buggy business. There was no battle with the thorns; with the throbbing reminder of her hand that her actions were within her control, she gave them space and acknowledged their place was where they were. Smiling, she imagined life was a Choose Your Own Adventure and decided she wanted to choose wisely.

Her experiences were her own, and she could rise above (or in this case, below) the fray of her environment if she so chose. "I simply need to be aware of what surrounds me, allow its role on my path, and discern the effect it has and how I feel about it. Easy! NOT," she said, with the pressure of the adventure in question increasingly dawning on her.

She paused in the moment as her last word landed like a brick on her spirit. This was her path to take, and easy or not, she was worth discovering. She believed her life was shaped by how she thought about things, and she knew that a shift in her thinking was a catalyst for change—maybe even THE catalyst for change.

The moment was upon her; her former life was shattered, and change was everywhere. She had been given this chance to discover her being. "And then I intend to start living it wholly," she declared to the universe with overwhelming gratitude.

She released the sarcasm with an exhale and breathed in to acknowledge outwardly, "It is up to me how I proceed at any moment. I may not like my choices, but I do *have* them, and for that I am grateful. I also want to feel good about how I behave and who I am in any circumstance. It is up to me to be the best me, and it all comes down to what I choose." Shaking her head with concession, she murmured to herself, "Whether it's meadows or marriages, it feels like the same lesson." Stella contemplated this thought for a few moments.

Beyond the edge of the skyline, she saw the tops of giant trees. They called to her being. Their grace invited her to come and sit beneath their canopy and rest in their shade. The idea immediately took hold in her mind.

The path phased from field to brush and was no longer lined with flowers as it transitioned upwards along a steep cliff wall.

Stella continued forth with new clarity and a jolt of life to her spirit. She'd been offered a lot to think about, which helped her find what was really behind her obstacles and how she could remedy it. *The Map Key is a compass within.*

It wasn't until she reached the end of the field that she realized the trees were not waiting for her and she would have to wait to rest under their canopy.

COBBLE STONE CORNER

Am I? I Am.

Stella was learning quickly that being present in this journey without assumptions or expectations would serve her well. This notion was validated by her disappointment—the trees were not where she perceived they were.

The expansive field quickly disappeared behind her as she proceeded on a narrowing path slowly changing from soil to crushed stone, requiring her to pay more attention to her footing. The environment was changing too. No longer broad and colorful, the hues became muted as a mountain wall began to take shape.

Mottled greens and whites of lichen-like plant life accentuated the patches of earth between rock and granite, creating a rising wall that seemed to skim her left shoulder as she walked, like the hand of a friend offering support. There was little sense of what was ahead, other than a bending hillside indicating for the first time that she was ascending.

As the long trail ahead unfolded and she became more comfortable with the terrain, she let her attention shift from rocks to birdsong; she could not see birds, but their songs filled the air. After a while, a distant call unlike any other lifted above the rest with a vibrant high pitch traveling from another place. She was overcome with the sense it was for her; it was a serenade in harmony with the birds. It was penetrating her inner core and vibrating her whole being.

Her ears activated to perceive the entrancing melody that was coming into tune. The tune was soon accompanied by words in a language she'd never heard, speaking of wonders unseen. She felt their meaning without understanding, and it was creating an energy that quickened her steps. Her curiosity engaged, and she shifted her focus to finding the source of this stunningly beautiful song.

Despite her new intentions, it was difficult to move forward without losing her step. She felt strong and capable and wanted so much to proceed expeditiously, yet the moment of desire was conflicting with her physical ability. Obstacles tended to frustrate her, especially at the end of a rather exhausting day, and she sensed herself slipping into that mindset. The more she hurried herself, the more she slipped back.

Recalling her reactionary, self-induced anxiety attack in Flutter Field, she slowed a bit and stopped pushing. With each breath, between each step, she released self-created obstacles within while moving steadily forward to the next spot. No longer trying to balance on one foot at a time, she found her center and began to balance herself from her core.

She felt her abdominal muscles tighten above her belly button and below her solar plexus; it was a peculiar spot. As she searched for it through some movement, she realized it sat within her light, the little glowing ball of self-awareness and the last bit of self she had nurtured and protected through loss. "It makes sense," she said out loud, "The muscles that hold my core physical being tall and strong are in the same place as my soul's light. The strength of my spiritual being holds me up in the same way."

With this connection, she was able to move forward more easily, with her eyes looking ahead instead of down in anxious fear of stumbling. When she inevitably missed a step, instead of frustration, a bubble of silliness brought lift to her feet. It reminded her to not take it all so seriously and relax. A smile came to her face, which immediately lifted her yet again. *A smile lifts more than the corners of your mouth*, her inner voice quipped.

At this point she was almost gliding, moving *along* the surface and impacted very little by the ridges and cracks, slips and slides as if carried by the music that still blanketed her mind. Now, *SHE* felt buoyant.

As she reached what seemed to be the first turn to switchback in the other direction and continue up the face of the mountain, the path seemed to vanish at the bend. It was just far enough that she had to squint to try to see beyond it. It was then she noticed a hazy figure ahead.

She could not yet see anything but the silhouette of a person she was walking towards. It stood in the shade on the edge of a forest filled with lanky trees that allowed speckled light to flicker against the leaves, creating reflective medallions as the breeze tossed them about. There was a sense of comfort that washed over Stella, and the song she was following began to grow more intense as she focused on it.

Stepping closer, she stumbled again, over a rock she wasn't looking for. She went from floating to face down, and before she knew it, Stella was back on the ground. It was then that the music stopped and a gentle message came through to her: *Your missteps matter.* Holding onto her elevated mood while getting up, she dusted off the sense of embarrassment with the debris of the path and did not let it distract her from her destination.

Her heart raced as she got closer. She felt an inner push to connect to the stranger ahead. She let go and trusted her awareness; after all, the talking fish said to. In the last few steps before she reached the stranger, Stella's inner voice spoke up to say:

Spiraling Up

> I am lighthearted.
> I am at ease.
> I am insightful.
> I am present.
> I am moving forward.

All of it was more than she could say just a short time ago. "Hello!" Stella called out, waving ahead to what appeared to be a woman sitting on a boulder. She gleefully waved back and said, "Come join me for a moment!", motioning her hands towards Stella. Nodding with approval, Stella headed her way with a new sense of excitement.

The woman welcomed Stella to sit, with eyes that smiled like a child, letting her know she was no longer a stranger. Stella found a few ledges on the side of a waist-high rock and was able to easily step up to her. "I am Madam AuraCull Văzător," she said in a much deeper voice than the soprano pitch of the song Stella heard. "I am so pleased to meet you at last." She had a grit and a wisdom to her voice that seemed to absorb the gravity Stella had released to be able to reach her.

With a glint in her eye and a sly smile, Madam AuraCull continued after Stella's introduction, "Welcome, dear one. I am a Văzător, one in a long line of seers, knowers and guides. It is my gift for channeling that invited you to find me. You are on a fantastical journey in which you build what's next from now with intention, discernment and connection. Listen to what calls you, feel the sensations that come to your awareness and trust your intuition. You are learning to understand what you already know."

Realizing again the magic of this place, she forewent the pause of wondering how this woman could know to say such a thing to her. She simply honored her words by responding with, "Thank you for sharing your wisdom. I am only just beginning to know where I am and how to discern what that means, and I have no idea where I am going," and ended with a humble sigh.

"PERFECT!" the woman laughed, "That's the best place for a new adventure to begin!" As her eyes lit up, her laughter seemed to bounce between the boulders and trees, echoing abundant joy in full surround sound. With a smile, Stella settled into the woman's words surprisingly easily and quieted to take in this magical moment. After a bit of silence, Stella was still settling on the boulder, trying to find a comfortable spot to sit when Madam AuraCull began to channel again.

She started to chant in her middle register, with pulsing breaths and heaving tones as if the air were being compressed out of her. Her thrusts came with force and weight and oomph—it was not light like the gentle melody that drew Stella in. As Madam AuraCull chanted, Stella became settled into the rock.

She noticed it was no longer hard and achy on her backside; rather it nestled around her like that perfect spot on a sandy beach that conforms to your unique shape. She did not notice the rock actually moving, which was what she half expected given this unique mountain so far. Stella simply felt more comfortable than she had a moment ago, and with that quiet awareness, the chanting stopped.

"Excuse me, Madam AuraCull," Stella queried, "Can you share with me what you are channeling? Your voice is so varied. I am intrigued by the sounds and the way they enchant me. Please, can you tell me about them?"

"You first heard the voice of Kuan Yin. She lightened your steps with a song that is sweet and airy on the breeze. If your thoughts call you to connect, you become a conduit for her divine energy, messages and love. Kuan Yin is a goddess of compassion and kindness. She is grace, and she guided you to lift your mind and lead your thoughts to see all you are, with compassion for self, to lighten your heart and steady your way. Connecting to Kuan Yin will help you rise above the fray." Her words came with a visceral resonance of truth. Stella muttered a "wow"; what was just described was exactly what she had experienced while traveling that bumpy trail.

Madam AuraCull continued, "Gaia then offered a chant for your comfort, sweet Stella. It is because of her that we are sisters, for she is our Mother Earth, the Guardian of Nature and the goddess of all that is earthly bound. She embodied the voice of the stone, to allow you to find comfort in what is, instead of trying to change it. Binding with rock, she guided your mind to find ease in the way things are in this moment, naturally, organically; for we are all one, even with this boulder that we rest upon."

Quietly stunned by how incredible this moment felt, Stella had no words of her own. It was like hearing from a long-lost friend whom she missed terribly, though this woman was previously unknown. Stella's heart felt huge, and her eyes welled up. She once again found herself holding on to Madam AuraCull's hand; she wasn't really sure if she had ever let go.

"On this journey, you will discover the answers to many questions, even those unasked. You will face obstacles you did not know you had, and you will find parts of you that were forgotten long ago. The journey life offers us is full of choices. It may not start off that way, and plenty of it feels like there's nothing to choose, but there always is. If nothing else, our thoughts are always our own. And as you have done today, your thoughts can lift, connect, ease and guide you to places in your mind, your heart and your world that simply make the journey better. In fact, your thoughts are the most impactful choice of all."

Stella was streaming tears. They just flowed of their own accord in response to the overwhelming feels flooding in. She conceded,

"I'm beginning to believe it really is that easy," without the sarcasm this time.

"Yes, dear Stella, it really IS that easy."

Stella sat quietly, absorbing it all until a wash of readiness came over her. With a last squeeze of Madam's hand and a thousand words contained in a glance, she let go of her grip. She then rose from the stone and prepared to step down from the boulder. "Wait!" Madam called out, "Kuan Yin has another gift for you," and plunged into a satchel behind her that Stella hadn't noticed.

She reached towards Stella and placed a small vessel in her hand that was shaped like a raindrop of glass with a stopper at the top. Its contents swirled like liquid pearls. "Kuan Yin is the guardian of where land and water *meet*. She harnesses the wisdom and force of the universe to protect those who wander on *both*. Sometimes we end up walking the in-between, which can be a muddy place. When in the muck, Kuan Yin's Pearls of Illumination will help you find your shimmer."

Overtaken with gratitude, Stella reached up and accepted the gift. Despite the glass vial appearing as delicate as any she'd ever touched, it felt sturdy and unbreakable in her hand. It was a beautiful mystery that she graciously placed in her pocket.

"One last thought from my spirit, sweet Stella…YES!" As her whole body jumped up to stand high where she had been sitting low, with exuberance her arms spread wide and she said, "Do yourself a favor and say YES! Whenever you know it's not a no."

"Say yes?" Stella repeated, looking up. "Yes!", Madam exclaimed with laughter, "*Yes* opens doors to new adventures! Oh, and…" She leaned down toward her and said with a hushed tone, "If you don't know if you want to say yes, ask yourself if the answer is no. Surely, one of those questions will open your awareness and guide your choices to create your path of desire. Life is a Choose Your Own Adventure, dear Stella. Choose intentionally!"

Feeling validated for having a very similar thought not long ago, Stella chose to give all of this insight some time to sink in. She quietly stepped backwards onto the rocky path, looking at Madam AuraCull still and waving fondly to this mysterious and magical woman.

Stella finally turned, and a few yards down the way, she heard a final faint call: "Carry on to the caravan and they will care for you!" And with that, Stella was on her way to find her next yes.

THE CARAVAN
A Mobile Service with Great Reception

Not long after leaving Madam AuraCull, the landscape again opened up to a flattened field, but unlike the last, it was full of other people milling around a collage of diverse and well-traveled wagons. "This must be the caravan she spoke of," Stella said to herself.

She was first greeted by flags flapping in the breeze, then an archway of curly willow branches with a handwritten banner welcoming entry to all who drew near. Stella skipped towards the field, light and joyful. She quickly got close enough to smell something cooking and realized she was famished.

As soon as she entered the community, she was greeted by a woman, short in stature with platinum blonde hair that piled on top of her head with a fork to hold the loose bun in place. A single word rolled generously off her tongue, tempting of things to come, "Welcome." Wearing an apron dusted with flour, tied below her breasts, she smelled of caramelized onions and roasted meats, which immediately made Stella's mouth water.

Inundated with the aroma of a well-loved kitchen, "Yum," was all Stella could say in reply as she was promptly overtaken by her hunger. "No better compliment to be had!", the hostess responded as she reached for Stella's hand and guided her to the first wagon. On the side of the wagon, an awning hung over an open space, brimming with vivacity. Bubbling, sizzling, snapping and crackling; each of the sounds made Stella's cravings even stronger.

"Did you know that YUM is the sound of the heart chakra?" the mystic chef inquired. Stella shook her head no. "Every YUM opens the heart, connects the spirit and feeds the soul, so thank you for greeting me with the most perfect hello I could ever receive," she spoke with a smile that revealed a single tooth missing from the front and center of her timeless face. Reflecting the warm grin, Stella came back with, "I had no idea! Now I will say YUM to everything that makes life delicious."

Nodding her approval, Stella's host offered her a spoonful of what was bubbling in the pot. With the first drip on her taste buds, Stella's eyes opened with delight, and she boldly said, "Yes, please!" Then she suddenly retreated with, "I'm sorry, I didn't even know I was hungry until the fragrance of your feast wafted my way. I have no money to buy a meal."

"Then you shall repay me with your company." The offering came with a glint in her eye while filling a bowl.

Stella was invited to sit at her hearth, where a series of curved benches surrounded an inviting fire a few yards away from the awning. Stella sat facing the kitchen and was handed a serenade of aromatics in a hearty bowl of stewed root vegetables in bone broth, something her hostess called "Troll food." "Chunky, hearty and organic, it changes every day, evolving with every fresh ingredient I add to the pot. I hope you can taste the love. It serves my soul to nurture yours," the woman proudly spoke of her specialty. Stella responded without lifting her head from the bowl, "My belly is warm, my heart is full and I can surely taste the love. Thank you, thank you, thank you," she earnestly gushed between bites.

The hostess sat beside her, sipping a cup of tea from a dainty mug. While eating, Stella observed this woman's distinctive beauty. Her clothes were layered and colorful, a mismatch of patterns and textiles that burst with life like a spontaneous party on the beach. Her hands were worn from work and seemed to know of the value they brought to the world through their actions. Stella felt enriched by this woman, not just by her food, and began to slow her dining to a practical pace. At last, she put the spoon on the edge of the bowl, gave a sigh of contentment and finally introduced herself.

"Please forgive me. I hope I wasn't rude. The aroma you created was so tempting, I was unable to do anything until I indulged in your delicious offering." A bit embarrassed still, she reached out for her hostess's hand and said, "I am Stella, and I am honored to sit at your hearth," bowing her head in gratitude.

"Ah, Stella," she replied, "Rude? Not at all, my dear," tapping her hand on Stella's in reassurance. "Watching others enjoy the food I create nourishes my spirit. I am FannySi," she expressed with a giggle, "It sounds like fantasy, a bit of which I may be." With a coy wink, she continued, "I am a Faerie in human form, which is not the Faerie norm. *Shee* is me, spelled S I D H E. The D is silent," she said with a wink, "I am an ancient spirit and I offer my blessings to nurture yours."

"I feel like I have been given a bonus life in a video game!" Stella rejoiced over the meal, "I feel amazing!" With a look that mimicked an actor receiving the anticipated award of a lifetime, "Yes," said FannySi, well aware of her gifts, "That's wonderful! I am grateful you enjoy it so much." Then with a pause, she added, "Faerie food binds the one who gives and the one who receives. Did I mention that? When you enjoy my food freely, it connects us indelibly." "That seems like a blessing," Stella replied, without giving much thought to what a binding connection to Sidhe might mean. "We are bound in YUM,

Spiraling Up

Stella, where delicious meets love. FannySi is safe, you see, but let the Faerie lesson be. Know with whom you partake and you may avoid a big mistake."

"It's a cautionary tale for another day," she muttered before Stella could respond. With a clasp of her hands at her heart, FannySi lit up her eyes, widened her smile and calmly tilted her head forward with a humble nod, letting out a sweet "blessings be." They sat a few moments longer until FannySi was called to service; she got up, adjusted her apron and headed back towards the stockpot with a welcoming grin on her face.

Sitting quietly with her back to the fireside, Stella's eyes lifted from her bowl. It wasn't until then that she had expanded her vision of her surroundings, as she had only managed to get a few feet within the caravan before stopping and feasting on the fantastic meal. Stella felt content.

The next thing that caught her attention was the sound of a gathering nearby. The sound was behind her, so she spun around on the bench, facing the fire, and spotted a crowd gathered a few wagons away. In the dimming light of day, she saw a man who seemed to be about 7 feet tall! His stately figure elegantly swayed, eyes closed, head facing the sky and hands pointing up as a floor for his fingers to dance on.

He bounced as he spread joy to those watching; she could see on their faces and feel it from where she sat. He was singing a song too. The melody was catchy, but Stella couldn't make out the words. When she released her attention from the show, she brought it to the fire and realized she wasn't there alone. Was he there the whole time? She leaned shyly towards him and offered a greeting. He offered a kind reply, and Stella then asked if he knew what was happening further down the path.

In the space between her query and his ensuing response, she noticed the man was holding a glass filled with crystals instead of ice. They created a sparkle from the firelight that flitted across him. He was a man unlike any, truly captivating. Stella was charmed by his presence. His body was fit, his stature poised, and he had skin that was sun-drenched and polished like a stone on the river's edge. She kept hearing the word YUM in her thoughts and got a thrill out of the fact that it was no longer about the food.

She couldn't look away from him. She was mesmerized by the way the light climbed up his body, flickered along his chest, then highlighted his lips and cheekbones until it found its way up to his evergreen eyes and then poured itself in. Was she staring? Who was this guy? She was flush.

His energy felt like it came from the earth, grounded and ancient but with the childlike wonder she was encouraged to embrace. She was immersed in his radiance. His long sun-bleached dreadlocks were neatly bundled and tied with various bands of beads that dangled over the edge of a blanket loosely draped upon his shoulders. The visceral reaction she felt upon his sight was unexpected; it had been a long time since anything had inspired it. She felt demure.

This stranger clearly witnessed her affect and eventually turned to her with a smile that would stop a clock; if she had been wearing pearls, she would have clutched them. "Hello, love. We have yet to meet," he extended his hand to greet hers for a cordial introduction.

A gentle touch amplified the titillation, and all the zeal she was sending to him reflected back on her. It awakened her feminine energy, and she became well aware of its power in this moment. Her sudden self-adoration compounded and her own energy soon balanced his charisma. The effect was divine equality and at once she was present and relaxed.

Once they let go, she saw an earnest man behind the shimmer, her vision no longer filtered by dancing flames. She was now looking at the same man—minus the magnetism he had initially inspired in her. It seemed like he was getting ready to tell her a story.

"I am Dirt," he started. A perplexed look swept over her face, shaped by curiosity, surprise and enchantment. "Dirt?" she questioned, thinking that his glistening smile, sun-kissed skin and golden essence seemed disconnected from his name.

As if knowing her thoughts again, he leaned in and said, "I chose this name as I wandered the earth in search of my destined path. I didn't know where I was going, only that it lay ahead, and every step I took, I found gratitude in the simple awareness that I was moving forward."

Her attention was unwavering, and he continued, "Some days, life was like walking on cobblestones. Every step was wobbly. This way, that way—watch those ankles! Truly, there are rocky roads in life, and the ability to traverse them towards stable ground matters. Every tumble can contribute to your strength…if you let it."

His eyes wandered down to the ground as he kicked the soil about. "Some paths are slippery. I never could get my footing and just fell down and over and any which way. Those paths tested my patience and perseverance the most. When I get frustrated, I can't solve anything! It takes discernment to know which steps are safe and which ones may land you on your ass." He paused to chuckle and refresh with a sip of his drink.

"So, let me wrap this up for ya. Once I found solid ground, I never wanted to leave it. I found a place to rest my weary soul, and as I lay there, with my head on the earth at the edge of the woods much like where we are now, I saw my path."

Stella still silently absorbed all she could from him. He continued, "What is dirt?" And her mind again grappled with how NOT dirty he was. "It's the solid foundation upon which all is built!" Thrusting his hands away from his body, he was clearly enjoying the retelling of his aha moment.

"Dirt supports life. It is sturdy and shapeable, and it holds a microcosm of creation beyond the naked eye." She watched as he came back into himself, quieting his voice and movements while he summarized, "And that's who I am, thereby, ergo, and so on and such…I am Dirt." And with that, he lifted his crystal cup as if to cheers the universe for bringing him this realization.

Stella took a deep breath and, with a warm smile, replied, "Well, hello, Dirt! I am Stella," and she thanked him for sharing his story. She then sat quietly absorbing the wisdom in his words, words that reflected the Madam's guidance earlier, validating yet again her own awareness of what she was being guided to understand and integrate into her own being: *Find your footing and calm your mind, and your path will be revealed.*

After a few moments, Dirt pointed to the man attracting all the attention down the way that she inquired about earlier and blurted, "THAT is MacA AyA. He sings of the stars." He then reached into his pocket and flipped Stella a small object to catch. "You asked about the festivities over there. I suggest you check them out when you are ready." Then Dirt went quiet again and sipped from his cup, settling into the earth in quiet repose by the fire, and his eyes slowly closed in solitude.

She wasn't sure why Dirt had tossed the token her way, but she assumed she would find out shortly. The daylight was fading as Stella quietly left his side, rinsed the empty supper dish she was still holding in a nearby wash station and headed up the path towards the festivities. With a happy tummy and a full heart, she was inspired by Dirt's

Spiraling Up

self-awareness and ability to be who he was meant to be on his own terms. She felt empowered.

What she caught seemed to be a coin, matte black—but not. It was about two inches around and heavy for something its size, with a dark deep gray color and coarse texture. Like a pumice stone but much denser, it felt to her like it had its own gravitational pull when it was in her hand.

As she looked closer, she noticed the crevices had sparkles in them; she wondered if there were hidden elements within. There was also writing on it. Though it was hard to see in the present light, she could feel the embedded letters that encircled the coins edge. A centered word was also etched into the surface on either side. Pausing in the tender light of newly lit torches, she could see the one side said *RICH*, and the other said *RACE*.

DOUBLE R STARBIT - A Rare Coin Indeed

MacA AyA stood taller than anyone she'd ever seen. He towered before the crowd, draped in a cream-colored shirt that contrasted with his shoulder-length dark hair. He wore patchwork pants made of every color imaginable, quilted as if they'd been extended for years to match his ever-growing height. Everything about him said *free spirit*. His joy was expansive, his energy exuberant, and he drew a gathering of folk wide-eyed and eager to hear what he had to say.

Looking up, Stella saw her first evening sky in this magical place. She paused in that moment to take in the starscape. The billion specks of light peeking through a blanket of black sky reminded her of the coin. The stars were distant, yet so present, it felt like they too were watching MacA AyA.

He sang, and his hands swayed in the form of upward-facing cups. Electrical quirks jolted him into random contortions on his cheek, his eye, his finger, his shoulder and his arm in a series of twitches. It looked like a flow of impulses running though his body, with no signs of distress. When the singing had stopped, Stella was considering heading down the path again, but then he took a deep breath, gave thanks to the great beyond, relaxed his body and made eye contact with the people around him. She waited to see what would come next.

He started to speak in contexts bigger than any one person, calling to the gathering for validation of their intentions. "Do you seek light and love?" The crowd nodded and mumbled in agreement. He asked again more intently, encouraging a bolder response. "YES!" the people cried out with such gusto, Stella's heart skipped a beat. She sensed the crowd knew something she didn't about this guy.

She was still only a curious passerby, not ready to grab the yes, nor willing to say it was a no. She stayed to the back of the crowd as it all seemed a little dramatic, and she wasn't sure if it was for her. She quietly observed as she tumbled the newly gifted coin between her fingers. "Love is infinite," he said, and his words landed on her with the weight of history.

Spiraling Up

In her life, Stella had searched for unconditional love and never felt she found it. She came to believe it was an illusion…or delusion. Too often, there was a threat of having love taken from her if she did not comply, behave or rise to someone else's needs before her own. *Infinite*, she pondered, *is vast and never-ending. It does not die. Energy does not cease to exist, and love is pure energy of the highest kind. Love IS infinite.*

Connecting to that feeling of expansiveness felt warm and humbling. It opened her mind to the loves of her life. Her body was recalling the warmth of comfort and care, the sparkle of affection and the lightness of heart that accompanied love, even when fleeting. These feelings weren't all connected to people; the purest love she could recall was with a pet. She felt blessed to know those feelings, and they began to wrap her like a familiar hug.

Her attention diverted back to MacA AyA's words: "Infinite love lives in flow, to and fro." They were rhythmic and vibratory, and projected through a smile tall and wide. "With love of self, you are never without love! Be the energy of love and accept it in return. When you do, the power of the universe is within you." Tears ran down Stella's cheeks.

MacA AyA fell quiet for a moment. His brow lowered for the first time since she had seen him. In a tone of earnest truth, he slowly and deeply said, "From love, there is joy, and from joy, there is ease. Release the obstacles in your life, open the possibilities and allow the light of love to brighten all that darkens your world."

He held up a coin that matched Stella's, except it hung as a pendant from his neck on a long silver thread. He called it "the Double R Starbit." He then grabbed a strap that was across his chest and spun it around to reveal a large fabric tote of many colors. He reached in and began to offer anyone interested a coin of their own as a "token of grace," a gesture of benevolence. As he spoke, she saw in nearby light that the side of her coin read the words he had just uttered: *Love is joy. Joy is ease.*

"The letters on each side of the coin are a gift of expeditiousness from the universe. Each side of the coin is a reminder of your own strength and a way to create a conscious life on your chosen path." He continued, "*RICH* is so much more than wealth, and *RACE* is not about identity or competition—each is an acronym meant to help you focus your intent so you may progress on your path."

"HOW?" Stella blurted out from the edge of the crowd, surprising herself that she was now a participant. In unison, and for the first time, the people moved their eyes from MacA AyA and they were suddenly upon her. He could see she was startled by her own inquiry and moved towards her through the crowd. The people looked like tall strands of grass, bending their movement to allow for his.

In a moment, they were face-to-face. She hadn't seen his eyes until now. They sparkled like a galaxy swirling of color and starlight. She was instantly entranced. She held out her hand to show him her coin. He then placed his hand on hers and spoke to her directly, though loud enough for all watching to listen and learn: "For Clearing," he said, "R is for *Release,* I for *Integrate,* C for *Clear* and H for *Harmonize.*" He asked her to close her eyes and feel the words on the coin with the *RICH* side up.

"Can you think of anything you'd like to clear from your path? Barriers to your journey or thoughts that no longer serve you?" he asked Stella. A rush of possibilities spilled into her thoughts but not across her lips; instead, she meekly nodded yes. "Excellent!" he dramatically replied, not needing any specifics to continue, "Repeat what I say: *Everything that allows me to be affected by the past in a way that no longer serves the present or future, RICH.*" She did as he instructed.

Spiraling Up

"Now," he said quickly, still focused directly on her, "There are two sides to every coin. Let's flip it. RACE is for Creation: R is for Radiate, A is for Activate, C is for Create and E is for Expand...Can you think of a shift for the better that you seek?" he inquired. "Ease and flow of the good stuff," she somehow managed to say.

He encouraged her again to repeat after him, "We call in ease and flow of the good stuff to show up as if by magic. All that blocks my path, RICH. And all that aligns my focus and creates this path, RACE!" He reverberated his message in a powerful, emphatic, booming voice. Then, in an instant, he was calm and finished with a subdued "Reality Reset."

As she finished her clearing with *RACE*, to her shock, she felt an energetic *WOOSH!* wash over her as if a cool breeze suddenly refreshed her from head to toe. She had goose pimples! It was a delightful shiver that gave her a sense of being heard.

She opened her eyes as he let go of her hand and turned to walk back to his place at the front of the gathering. She quietly finished with "Reality Reset." *WOOSH!* She felt a rapid surge of energy flow through her again.

Now facing the crowd, MacA AyA gleefully yelled out, "Remember *Reality Reset*! It will reset your present with a past that is cleared and released with RICH, and with all that you created and expanded with RACE! When you use it, the molecules of Infinite Consciousness shift, allowing everything in your reality to function from this new place." He laughed joyfully as if that all made perfect sense and began to interact graciously with his inspired and enlightened patrons.

He opened the side door of his caravan and revealed seating for two. Here he offered private sessions to anyone interested in more as people began to approach him. Stella stepped away from MacA AyA's teachings energized, untethered and uplifted, and that was enough for her. She was now ready for ease and flow, excited to say YES to the next bit of good stuff. Coin in pocket, she headed down the trail lined with flickering lanterns hanging upon the wagons.

Not all were bustling; in fact, many were darkened with shades drawn. Some carried quiet songs of long days, while others had small gatherings of what looked to be family and friends sharing meals and relaxing for the night. It was all very comforting to Stella. Though she was only passing through, she felt part of a collective.

The wagoners radiated an abundance of grace that flowed from their traveling homes. It was a delightful community she was grateful to have encountered, and it was nice to not be alone. She sensed their conscientious choices to tread lightly, carry little and leave no trace. She was picking up on a mood that felt burden-free, easygoing and light, and it inspired her to imagine how she could integrate that vibe into her life too.

Further down the path she heard music wafting from between two wagons. Pausing to peek through, she saw folks sitting around a firepit singing, dancing and relaxing with merriment. There was a strumming guitar, a sweetly humming viola and someone drumming on a wooden box; it was a great groove.

She wasn't inclined to join, though she felt she would be welcome. The music inspired a sway in her body and a swing in her arms. Focused on the rhythm, she returned to the path with a shimmy in her walk until she finally gave in and found herself leading a dance procession of one. She felt unencumbered.

Stella could feel her body release its structure into a fluid state; no more hard corners, just soft edges. She wondered why she couldn't always move forward with this type of easy motion; it felt so different from the methodical pace she took sometimes when she just carried forward. When music captured her spirit, she knew it had the ability to cause her to shift mentally, emotionally, and spiritually—yet she hadn't thought of it as a catalyst for change. Following along with the chorus of a song she only just heard, she sang, "Once you know, you can't unknoooooooooow!" like a rock star. She celebrated the significantly insignificant aha moment wholeheartedly; a tiny flash of awareness with a big ripple effect.

She could no longer hear the music but didn't stop dancing. She walked and danced to her own melody as it created her flow, and in that moment, she became aware of the contrast between how it felt to be drudging through the muck and how it felt to be simply gliding over it. Stella "Reality Reset" the moment, not just to lock in her words, but also the melody. "Why not?" she sang to herself, still dancing. She felt groovy.

She had slowed her dancing to a waltz when she saw what would be her next destination up ahead. A woman sitting alone at a table for two waited beneath a small window with a perfect reflection of the moon. As Stella approached her, she saw the glassy sign that read *Lady JuJu.*

"Good evening, traveler. Will you join me?" she offered as she gestured to the empty chair. "I am Lady JuJu, and the library is open." "Thank you," Stella replied as she sat down, "You have a library? Where are the books?"

"I am a reader of the Akashic Records, the library of the universe. I can open your book and read from your pasts, futures and nows." With questions already spinning in her head, Stella decided upon one: "You said plural—pastS, futureS and nowS? How can that be?"

"You have lived many lives before this one, though you likely don't remember. You have existed before, creating many pasts. You have lived many selves within this life, have you not? These are your many nows. And you surely have discovered that you can shape your life in any moment of the present, which means any moment can create new futures. Does that make sense?" Nodding in agreement, Stella realized that somehow that did make sense.

"Did you know you could be allergic to flowers because in a past life you died in a field? It's true! Knowing who you've been helps you understand who you are and reveal new ways to be who you were born to be."

There was a new luminescence at the table, no longer just the moonlight reflecting down. It was emanating from Lady JuJu. She was literally radiant; glowing from within as she called in the guides most helpful in this moment.

"If you would like me to look at your records, simply speak your full name." Upon Stella speaking her name, Lady JuJu perked up and exclaimed, "Yes! I see it. Your book is strongly bound and abundantly notating your soul's history. OH..." she interjected herself with something distant. In the next moment, she took a firmer tone. "There is something holding you back, a pocket of grief stitched to the back of your heart. It's painful. It is scar tissue from an old emotional wound. Removing it will help your path ahead. This is why we see it now. May I remove it for you?" "Yes please," Stella said.

Lady JuJu stood up and walked around the table, running a finger from Stella's hand, up her arm, over her shoulder and down her back to a spot just below her shoulder blade. Stella was facing away and could not see what Lady JuJu was doing, but for some reason, Stella had a vision of a puffball mushroom sitting hidden behind her heart.

Lady JuJu slowed her fingertip and said, "Right here." She then pressed down as if pushing a button. Stella felt the touch upon her mid back and POOF! The puffball burst, releasing an explosion of microscopic, dehydrated pain, and the results were simultaneous.

Stella's eyes exploded a waterfall of tears, and her cheeks pulled back with a huge smile. She was overcome with release and relief. "I am crying! And laughing! What's happening?!" she chirped through a confused chuckle. They both let out a bold guffaw; Stella for the confusing, unexpected and overwhelming reaction, and Lady JuJu as witness to the delightful moment.

As they both giggled, Stella let the tears roll off her face while Lady JuJu returned to her seat. Not wiping her tears away became practice for Stella in grief. Her falling tears became armor, like a shield that encased her if she felt vulnerable. It was a full body embrace of emotion, something that started one evening when sitting still lost in tears. She felt them fall from her cheeks and land on her bare feet, and the sensation was so powerful, she never again wiped them away. Tears didn't stop her from feeling joy in this moment either; actually, they intensified it.

The Caravan

She found something in a hidden pocket.

Spiraling Up

In the pause after laughter, Lady JuJu offered a bit more: "On this path, you will face beauty, joy and connections you have never imagined. There will also be difficulties and moments that feel lonely. Do not fear the wisdom each of these moments will give you." Echoing Fredrico's words, she added, "Trust you are safe, for this is a path built on love. It is not a question of IF you will complete the journey, but rather who you choose to be as you walk it."

In a fluid singular movement, Lady JuJu reached her hand into the lantern on the table, pulled the flame out with a closed fist and extended it towards Stella. Following the physical cues, Stella turned her hands open palms up and prepared to receive this unusual gift, wondering if she was about to hold a flame.

She didn't wonder long as within a breath, she was holding a smooth, shimmering stone. Amid the sudden darkness upon the table, she could see opalescent striations of layers frozen in time within the stone as if they were fiberoptics.

The stone was a channeler. Lady JuJu called it LaLu Narock as she rested her hands in her lap and sat back to observe the introduction between two givers of light. It was evident how much she was enjoying it as a smile swept across her face and her fingers wiggled with delight.

Then she began to hum. When she did, LaLu Narock gradually glowed and then dimmed slowly as she stopped. "I was just saying thank you," she said as she glanced at the stone. "LaLu Narock will channel your light through its own into a radiant guide for you in dark places."

Stella was beside herself, overflowing with energy that resonated from her core and then bounced out to reverberate through her being. She felt herself shaking loose jagged bits, like gravel between her joints, as if the hidden walls within started cracking from exposure to a focused spotlight. She blurted out, "I'm tingling!" She felt effervescent.

"The helpers say this exchange is now complete. Thank you to the beings of light who have joined us this evening. Stella, your Akashic Records are now closed." Stella felt closure watching Lady JuJu end the session; she kept her eyes closed with hands cupped and lifted as she gave thanks for the clairvoyant conversations from beyond their table. The communion held so much gratitude, there was no doubt it could be felt across galaxies.

When her eyes opened, Stella spoke, "Lady JuJu, I can't begin to understand what we just shared here, or ever thank you properly for the experience. I have nothing to offer you but the clothes on my back and they are filthy, covered with mud and scraggly bits from the path I have taken here." "Mud?" she replied eagerly, "Did you happen to wade through a sticky bog?" "Yes," Stella replied. "Did you then wander through a field aflutter too?" Again, Stella replied yes.

Lady JuJu jumped out of her seat and began to dance a little happy dance. The reason why, Stella did not know. "Oh, Starlight, this is wondrous news! Would you bless me with another exchange? I sense you might desire. Will you please allow me to trade your clothing for a set of others?" Then, suddenly calm and looking Stella in the eyes, she gently added, "Please."

"Of course! I want to honor your generosity with some of my own in any way I can," Stella replied laughing, "but why in the world would you want my muddy clothes?" Already making a small pile of new garments for her to choose from, Lady JuJu began to speak of gardens. "I travel across many lands and over many mountains. The path is my home, and my tribe wanders with me, though sometimes only for a moment on a dark evening beside the wagon," she said, winking at Stella, kindly including their moment in her story.

"You have stumbled and fallen, risen and carried yourself through nature's finest offerings! Your attire is not simply muddy. You have

Spiraling Up

molded the rich soil, mosses, waters and seeds into compacted clumps of new gardens!" She looked absolutely giddy as she spoke. *Of course there's a metaphor here*, thought Stella, *about the compacted muck of life you carry and simply want to shed, unaware it may be the seeds for growth and beauty yet to come.* "Wow, that's a shift in perspectives," Stella then heard herself say aloud.

"Please see if any of these clothes suit you. If they do, step behind the curtain and you can change into them," which is exactly what Stella did. Focused on carefully removing the dried clumps from the garments, Lady JuJu began to make a small pile of it on the table. She then handed some back to Stella, suggesting she drop it along her path. "You see, as I travel, I leave my mark with a garden. A patch of joy in any given place, surprising those who pass with color, diversity, beauty and nourishment, like edible plants or a patch to rest and dream."

"Usually all I can do is drop a clump and know I may bring a smile to someone someday. Sometimes it is I who wanders by again with fond recognition as I gaze upon a season's display. Every now and then, I stay long enough to watch the vegetation grow and feed folks and critters as they pass by, rather than I." Stella noticed her speech gradually grow dreamier and dreamier.

"It is rare to be able to witness growth and experience another life from beginning to end, be it flower, animal or person. It is a gift. In passing or in place, you have rewarded me with the finest of offerings that I may leave on this good earth as I walk as one with many."

Stella was inspired by her words and renewed with fresh and comfortable clothes. She chose a sturdy pair of pants, patched with many pockets; one of them already full. A softly worn long-sleeve shirt, lightweight with just the right warmth for day or evening, finished off her new ensemble. As she came around the curtain she had changed behind, they both looked up and said, "Perfect!" in sync, though each for their own reasons.

As Stella prepared to leave, she inquired about a place to sleep for the night. "You have released stagnant pain. Hydrate and allow yourself to reset. Rest your head beneath the ancient Redwood, past the final wagon, on the other side of the path. She awaits you. Sleep well, sweet Stella, and thank you for brightening my evening." After an encouraging hug goodbye, Stella turned and, as guided, walked ahead towards a giant tree. Perhaps it was the same one that stood out to her from the fields. There was so much to absorb from the evening, just as Madam AuraCull said—they did indeed care for her at the caravan.

THE SAFE KEY

*Standing Strong with Deep Roots
Like the Tallest Tree*

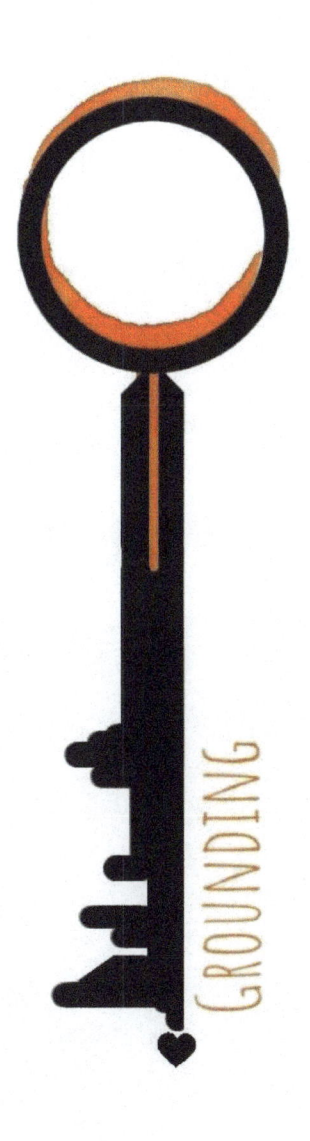

GROUNDING

ROOTS RUN DEEP
The Ancient Grandmother

Stella followed directions and wandered along the dimly lit path until it was lit no more. She sensed a cooling as the evening breeze drifted by without the row of caravans protecting her. Guided by the shadows of night, the shapes of the path and its plants caught the occasional reflection of flickering stars against waxy petals and delicate pools of water; it was enough for her to confidently make her way towards the next unknown.

Up ahead, the tree was clearly silhouetted by the twinkling sky. The slight variance of depth in the colors of midnight blocked by the towering Redwood created an indelible image of beauty in darkness.

Stella relaxed and found her pace quickening. As her stride became rhythmic, her rhythm became poetic. She tuned into her new chosen frequency. Without awareness, she began singing unfettered words from a place unknown in cadence with each step, now rapidly skipping towards the giant Redwood tree.

A bobble and a bit
A wobble and a wow
I am ready to stretch beyond
The heights and depths of now;
Singing with the Ancient Tree

Spiraling Up

Nature's tuning and alignment,
Your forests song's a symphony
Of blessings and enlightenment;
Grounded, aligned and open
Breathe my essence in;
From root to crown
And then back down
My clearing now begins;
Beneath the welcoming canopy
Your limbs move to and fro;
Connecting to your energy
I too am able to grow

With a huge smile and a glowing heart charged up by her playfulness, she stopped in her tracks at the end of the path and looked up. It was then that she met the Queen. Ancient tree indeed. From where she now stood, she could no longer see the top of this regal Redwood.

Deep, evergreen hues draped from each limb. Six-inch needles with the look of prickly pins were surprisingly gentle and inviting to touch. Each branch was curved and moved gently in the breeze, and as Stella's eyes followed them back, they swooped upwards and joined the massive trunk.

She was keenly aware of the power this tree held. Why Stella suddenly knew she was next to royalty she could not explain, but she was inspired to curtsy, so she did. Releasing any sense of ridiculousness, she leaned into what she felt was overwhelmingly true and worthy of honoring; the *hows* and *whys* did not matter.

Stella lifted her bowed head as she reached up and touched a branch now in front of her, as if grabbing the hand of another and greeting her with a formal introduction. Stella's mind became saturated with the name Queen Sequoia Braunston Browne, which left her shaking her head like there was a marble tossing about. She repeated audibly what she heard from within and was flushed with affirmation. Then came another connection: *I am your Ancient Grandmother.*

In that moment, the tree began to glow, outlined in amber light, the color of sap when the sun shines through it. She sensed the Queen was sharing the sensations Stella was feeling; they were communicating.

Stella walked beneath the canopy and could see why it was called a Redwood tree. The trunk was a reddish-brown color, rugged and yet soft, like timeless hand-dyed tapestry. The thick and fibrous bark frayed a burgundy cotton-like fluff, torn away by the abundance of wildlife this tree homed.

She walked up to the massive circumference, spreading her arms as wide as she could, and she was barely a quarter of the way around. She settled in and nestled the base of the abundant trunk. She relaxed into the cushiony ground at the base and lay down with her back against the Queen's towering strength. The amber glow returned and encased Stella in a cocoon of light.

The Ancient Tree was feeding Stella, like a grandmother often does, giving her what she needed to be strong. It was soup for the spirit, swirling with oxygen and nutrients, carried through mycelium and earth's energy, healing every cell and tenderly releasing all the aches in her traveling mind and body. The amber light was a salve for Stella's spirit; it was healing her light body too. Stella, unaware of all this in the moment, merely drifted to sleep, caressed by the organic sounds and gentle comfort that embraced her mind and began to fill it with loving thoughts of home.

"Welcome back," Stella heard as she opened her eyes. Surrounded by faded figures shrouded in gentle kindness, she was guided to relax

Spiraling Up

and get comfortable on a small sparkling slab nearby. The bench had a full spectrum of colors radiating beneath it, each one lit from a crystal pillar peering out like a joyful face in a window. As Stella lay down, three figures approached, silently sharing the words to speak when she was ready. "I am open to receive," said Stella, relaxing into the cold surface and closing her eyes.

SWOOSH! "I'm flying!" Stella yelled out, unwavering in her dream state. She realized she was hovering over herself and the three figures she now saw as small tree "people" with branches as arms and burled trunks that gave the impression of extraordinary faces. Behind them was the essence of the Queen Tree. Stella was again welcomed home by her Ancient Grandmother, from a lifetime eons ago. And the home, Stella was being told, was where her soul was happiest.

There were no words. The Ancient Grandmother was speaking in energy that traveled on swirls of amber and white light, emanating in waves and without need for interpretation. This dynamic movement was the face of the Queen Tree, and her meaning was fully understood with reverence.

The messages were coming in loud and clear. *Rise up to meet your tribe* was one. *Travel slowly with intention, compassion and high vibration* was another; Stella felt it as shivers. *Stay grounded* was yet another, accompanied by roots that began to grow from her feet. Looking up from them, she was offered a branch, held out vertically towards her, engraved with the words "Walk Steady with My Staff." This event was the preface to an overwhelming sense of connection and knowing that at any time she needed something, her ancient tribe was there for her among the trees.

Stella was overcome with warmth and comfort, and in a WOOSH, she was back on the slab. Her body pulsed with the words *infinite gratitude* within her like a rapid heartbeat. Just as she nodded to the little tree folk in acknowledgment, she was WOOSHED! backwards again into a clearing of stars and space and catapulted through time and the wisdoms of the ages. Oblivious to any of this, Stella's physical body, resting under the tree, began to shift about as her light body nestled back into its present home.

The Reunion

Stella was awakened by a tickle in her nostrils. It came from the forest's natural oils mingled with the morning dew. It misted her sympathetically like wild perfume. Stretching out the remarkably restful sleep, she felt refreshed and oddly different in the most agreeable way. As she looked upwards from her prone position, she could see the smattering of morning through the branches all the way up to the peak of the tree.

The animals within the canopy came to life, noisily peeking and pecking about while attending to their day full of duties. The birds chirped and the squirrels chattered as they scurried on every limb she saw. The songs were bold and bright. Each bird was notable and unique, yet it carried a synchronized portion of a greater tune, creating a forest symphony to welcome the day. Were they louder than usual? The sounds were practically high definition, she thought. Then she warmly recalled the Queen's messages. "Yes," Stella said, answering herself, *I am rooted in a higher vibration.*

"And grounded in infinite gratitude," she added, sighing deeply with a smile. Stella was listening.

Pondering her dream journey and whether it was a dream at all, she decided it didn't matter. Stella seemed to understand something new about the world. Her senses were altered; a bit more colorful, more fragrant, more resonant. She liked whatever it was. It felt uplifting and satisfying. She then realized there was no part of her that felt alone anymore.

As she began to sit up, she saw a pile next to her of nuts and berries beside an acorn cup with some type of syrup in it that carried scents of herbs and honey. Holding the cup between her fingertips, she offered it up to the air as a toast and enjoyed what were the tiniest sips ever. Despite the diminutive portion, it was ample. A greenish nectar that tasted of Chamomile, Wild Ginger and Orange Blossoms. Tiny or not, it burst of flavor and sweetly glazed her palate in the most delightful way.

The woodland offerings from unknown friends were happily nibbled on while thanking whomever, whatever and wherever they were for sharing. Stella had never felt so connected to the world around her as she did in this moment.

Within that sense of connection, there was awareness of her own direction. That connection gave her bearings again. What did the fish say? Answering herself out loud: "Calibrate my compass with the Map Key? Find the obstacles and clear my own path. Okay, I see that.

This must be what clearing my inner barriers feels like, opening space within, tilling the soil and preparing to plant my intentions for a new season of me!" Stella felt capable.

After she ate the treats, she discovered a small item at the bottom of the pile. It was hard like stone, yet looked like wood. It shimmered like diamond dust, and it was twisted like a climbing vine. One end looped, almost like a swirly number 2, and the other end was irregularly forked and blunt.

Curiously rolling it in her hands with a mesmerizing glare, she figured it had to be a key. *This must be the Safe Key*, she thought, remembering Fredrico's foretelling. It came with a sense of accomplishment, like she had made it onto the next level of this Choose Your Own Adventure journey. She found a long, thin strand of fibrous bark on the ground and looped it around the key to create a pendant, then placed it over her head to wear as a necklace, which reminded her of her latchkey kid days.

Now standing, she dusted the earth off of her and placed a hand on the trunk of the Redwood to honor and thank her. It was all too much for Stella to synthesize in the moment so she turned and quietly departed.

THE GARDEN PARTY

Frolicking in Another Dimension

Just before the main trail, a subtle path in the grass presented another option. As Stella glanced in its direction, she knew immediately it was hers to follow. The glimmer of the dew on the grass, the *come-hither* wisps of movement in the leaves and the light scent of beckoning flowers all called to her, so she went.

The grass was bright and slightly trampled on; she surmised it might be a path for deer. The trees were spread enough to let the sunlight through, which created mini gardens and vibrant patches of blooming color among the fallen needles and dried leaves. She reveled at the thought that this very greenery might have been seeded by Lady JuJu long ago.

The air was clean and light. She no longer smelled the flowers that had caught her attention earlier; instead, the smell was earthen and just warm enough to imply it was no longer morning. The path curved and rolled from side to side like a current in a stream. The moss became thicker, the ivy denser and the trees much, much older. She could tell by the girth of their trunks and the width of their canopies. They grew with their branches intertwined as if to say, "We are one."

One particular trunk stood out ahead, burled and gnarled, on which mushrooms grew like steps that climbed around and up as far as she could see. The ivy had overtaken a large portion and dressed it like a fashionable accessory, a draped swag across limbs that pooled on the ground like the train on a red carpet. Funny enough, the carpet of the old forest floor was *actually* red as the grass had been covered with fallen leaves.

As she approached the mighty trunk, she could see the bark was not simply bending, it was curving like an arch, and as she got closer still, she saw the outline of what looked to be a door. She caught her breath just before it escaped and widened her eyes, for certainly this must be where the key belonged. She reached out towards the ivy to shift around patches that were obscuring the arch and she saw it. Embedded in the bark was the shape of a door far taller than she, with curly little swirls of tree knots and ivy that looked just like the top of the key, in the shape of a number 2.

As it was no ordinary door, there was also no ordinary knob, or lock for that matter, and gaining entry was not going to be as simple as she hoped. She had no fear about what lay behind the door—she just wanted through it, so she persisted.

It became clear the door did not hold the lock, and once again, she found herself needing to step back to see the bigger picture. It was then that she noted a particular branch was a little sparkly. "AHA!" she giggled to herself, only just realizing that sparkles had been her clues all morning. She removed the key from her neck, and using one of the mushrooms as leverage, which was surprisingly sturdy, she stepped up and reached as far as she could towards a spot above the door.

A shadow image of the key was deeply embedded in the bark, and it began to glow as the key got closer. Stepping another mushroom up, she was able to reach it and the key connected as if joined by rare-earth magnets. A soft amber light traced the bark lines down to the top of the arch, then diverged to gently ease down each side. When it reached the surface of the ground, it too lit up, encompassing the place Stella stood. After a moment, the door became backlit with the same amber light and slowly became translucent.

Stella jumped off the shroom step and watched the last bit of the golden light reveal the hidden passage. Without hesitation, she walked through the door, then paused momentarily to look back. She clearly saw where she was standing, though there was no longer a glow from the forest floor. Stella turned again into the amber light within the tree and walked towards what looked to be a garden up ahead.

There were now walls along each side, covered in vining white flowers with tiny leaves and swirling branches; she thought *this must be what the key was made of.* She started to see dancing light up ahead, sparkles in the air like prisms in water, but it was not raining. It wasn't long until she saw the bouncing lights were Faeries. FAERIES?!

Her sensible brain flooded with, "No Way!", "This is real?" and "I am imagining it!" But she quickly shut that down because in this moment, she was bearing witness to what she always wanted to believe, and her heart was overflowing with joy. Her cheeks stretched so wide smiling that they seemed to open a portal to childlike wonder which quickly overtook her.

Moving ever closer, she saw the white light Faeries playing and rousing a creature she had never seen or imagined before. There seemed to be some sort of blue beast jumping and romping around like a puppy on a sunny day. In fact, it reminded her of just that, puppies and butterflies playing in a garden. She thought she could hear laughter, but the sounds were not within her realm and unfathomable; she could *feel* them laughing. She could feel the vibration and pulse of play lapping across her like the tide at the beach.

Watching them interact was the physical display of what she felt; words were not necessary. Smiling and laughing along with them, the creature eventually dropped down to lay on the soft garden bed and

Spiraling Up

the Faeries gently landed upon it. It was then that the amber eyes of the being lifted and looked directly at Stella, and with a deep, low, rumbly voice said, "I am Serophant, the Seraphim Dragon."

The melody of the introduction was celebratory and inviting. Stella felt more excited than anything, but somehow it wasn't surprising. *Of course there's a dragon and he is speaking to me,* she thought to herself while replying to him, "Hi, I'm Stella," waving like a schoolgirl meeting a new friend on the playground. "I know," he replied, "I've been waiting for you! Welcome to my garden in the heart of the Second Dimension." He continued to speak through giggles, "Where the Garden Party never stops!" And with that, he jumped, flicking all the Faeries up. After tumbling in the air, he began dancing around again.

Serophant

Stella had no idea how to process this new dimensional realm; the garden was almost cartoonish! It was an overload to her previously relaxed senses and quite honestly, she thought, *This is a bit much.*

Noting all that, she decided to enjoy the moment as it was and released her suspended reflection to laugh out loud at the absurdity and glorious wonder of it all. The more she allowed the fantastical to consume her mind, the deeper her belly laughs got. She then dropped to the ground and began rolling in silliness too. It was then that the glowing Faeries flew over and landed on her like dandelion fluff carried on a breeze.

In a pause for breath, she started to hear music, though she could not tell from where. Much like the laughter, it was more of a sensation than audible input. Serophant slowly walked up to Stella to gently nudge her up from the ground. As he guided her to sit next to him, he began to speak.

"This is Nature's Realm, where the conscious connection to Mother Earth resides. It connects us through the harmonious exchange of energy. We exist with you in your world, but if you do not connect to us in our plane, you won't be able to see us." Looking at Stella, he gave a gentle wink and a nudge of her arm with his long nose as if to say, *Am I being too subtle?*

Serophant continued, "This is a place of lightness, and there are many ways to find it. The quickest, and most fun, is play! When you play, you set your cares free, your heart and mind are open and your body pulses energy, clearing out what lays stagnant beneath the surface and replacing it with abundant, silly, exuberant joy!" Then, he gleefully did a backflip.

He spoke again: "You can also walk in the grass barefoot, breathe in the scent of a cedar tree, watch a dragonfly dance with a flower or feel the mist of falling water upon your face." Serophant added, "The splendor of this place is found in each and every one of these experiences, and so many more in nature. It's up to you to find which one brings you here."

Spiraling Up

Stella, speaking at last, asked if anyone else lived in this dimension, for she only saw him and the Faeries. He replied, "My Faerie friends bring light of all kinds to my world, and there are countless beings who live here. I, Serophant the Seraphim, am here to bring light to yours. It is I who you are meant to meet today, and I am honored to be your guide throughout the realms, if you'll have me."

"Of course!" she burst out, "It sounds amazing."

"Dearest Starlight, where you journey, I am. In any dimension, any time, I will be there to offer grounding in the most uplifting ways."

By now, the little light Faeries had begun to circle her, resting on her shoulder, her head, her hand. Little tingles sparked in accompaniment each time they landed. She could not see their details, only a pea-sized bit of light, which led to a random side thought: *Fairy lights! HA! They really do look like that.*

She brought her focus back to the talking dragon as he said, "It's nearly time for you to go, Stella. This realm is not a place for you to linger. Give time for playful, light and fun, because it's important for your best life. Ascension takes lift and nothing is quite as lofty as laughter!" and up he went, flipping himself and all the Faeries into the air with a flap of his wings.

Right as he landed, a wooden box appeared in Stella's hand that when shaken, rattled. She opened it up to find a set of unusual dice, not with numbers, but symbols. "Those are Qubes from the forests of my dimension," he said, "They are connected to the strongest source of energy: love. When you know how love flows, you can find joy much easier. When you play, love is there. When you laugh, that is the sound of love."

"When you dance, it is the beat of love. When you work, there is love in the care you give to yourself and others, so make work playful too! Any time you think of love, you generate more in the world, so *roll the dice and let love flow! Play is Joy is Love is Qubes.*" And with that, he walked up to her, smiled, then tapped her nose with a long golden tipped talon, and just like that, she was standing outside the tree in the forest alone.

It took a few moments to gather her senses; she felt dizzied, like she'd been spun around a few times before being set loose. Did she really just travel to another dimension? Was she hanging out with Faeries? Was that a blue dragon offering his services and dance moves? Before she could rationalize any of it, she realized not only did she have a box in her hand, but she was also wearing the key necklace once again. A smile reclaimed her face as she let her mind release the questions and simply hold glee and whimsy for the magical world she had just discovered.

Play more, she thought to herself. *Be love*, she nodded in awareness. "Carry joy," she exclaimed outwardly, "It's the lightest thing I will ever carry." She then finished quietly in her thoughts: *And the more I have, the lighter my burdens get.* Shaking her head as if it helped the widgets in her brain, she took a deep breath and started her way out of the woods towards the main path.

THE RESONANT KEY

Attune Discernment and Find Your Harmony

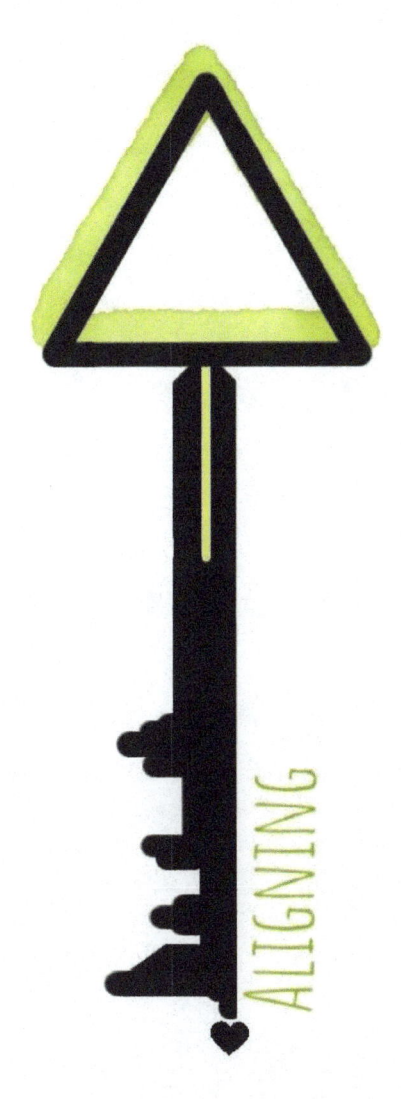

ALIGNING

RHYTHM RAPIDS

The Conductor

Coming down from the high of interdimensional travel, with the Qubes nestled into one of her pockets, Stella continued one step after the other on the path winding up the mountain. She noticed her frolic with Faeries left her feeling a bit discombobulated and her inner pendulum was swinging from awe to odd; she felt untethered.

Her focus moved to feeling grounded. She recalled the image of creating roots with every footstep that the Ancient Grandmother showed her. She was flushed with messages like *stand tall* and *be confident you cannot be felled.* The thought shift was working.

Stella felt grounded when she had a sense of being unshakeable and resolved in her own voice. She imagined the Redwood felt this way, even if variable winds tossed her about. When Stella believed in herself and carried her truth, she was powerful enough to hold her own, no matter whose winds pushed against her.

Winds of pressure that would push Stella away from her own center used to be the only force she knew. They were often produced by the words of those around her. Expectations, ultimatums and faults all tossed her around, sometimes with cataclysmic force. Believing she would not stand if not for their resistance, she was often exhausted just trying to exist.

She learned to find her own answers by making her own choices confidently before sharing what they were. If she spoke of her dreams and possibilities before then, they were often shot down, dismissed or even weaponized later against her. Sometimes random moments provided others the chance to prove to her how ridiculous those dreams were. All she really wanted was to be herself and feel accepted by those who said they loved her.

Once she discovered how to keep to herself and only share the tangible, it was much easier to hold her own among those who would diminish her. It was disheartening that the people who were supposed to be closest minimized her for their own needs. It never felt right and the weight of it became an anchor on her spirit.

Before she finished processing the side trip her thoughts took, she heard a message from deep in the woods: *I need you to find it.* This was external, not in her head, as far as she could tell. Stopping immediately, she spun around for the source. *A life such as yours should be kept in tune! Find the key your symphony is played in.* And on that note, it was gone.

At this point, she just took that in and carried on. She restarted her meandering self-talk and walk, and soon she approached a clearing. She was feeling aloof. "It's been a lot," she said to herself, "a lot a lot." She saw what appeared to be a little cottage off the main path and she headed towards it, wondering whether this was where that voice boomed from.

It was a squat tree house crafted from the base of what was once a massive tree with most of it long gone. It had a conical roof that was layered with life like an elevated patch of meadow. Tule fog rose from it as the sun crossed over the tree line behind Stella, creating a foggy halo above the cottage. It looked as if it was alive, loved and empty.

There was a doorway, though no door, cut through the outer few feet of the trunk. It led to a large room within the hollowed remains of this humongous tree. It was not clear how it had been hollowed, but it seemed a mixture of handwork and nature. To her right, the wall was scored with black embedded bolts that stretched out for several feet in many directions like upside down tree branches in silhouette; it was the mark of a lightning strike.

Her eyes wandered the room from there, slowly taking in the extraordinary space. The inside of the trunk walls were carved away into nooks and shelves, creating a lot of practical storage, which was being used to capacity. Overall, it was a sensible and functional space; quirky, cluttered and creative.

This was not a home, and it was too small for a gathering space; its purpose was still left to be discovered. She walked around the edge of the room and soaked in the majesty of it all. Everything was meticulously crafted, each piece of furniture and all that laid upon it. Even the papers were hand pressed from bark or plant fibers, and their markings were charcoal from a finely sharpened burnt stick. It was everything a mystical mountain cottage in a Faerie tale would be, complete with the mystery of the resident.

The room was warm, not in temperature but in temperament. She felt inspired and awakened in its presence as the sinking she felt earlier was losing its gravity. The room felt as if it was breathing, and she felt her own breath begin to synchronize into a stable, deep rhythm in and out. She began to feel at ease again, guided by a palpable resonance in the room. She felt grateful.

Still gingerly circling the room for clues of the occupant, she discovered music written on the stacks of pages layered along a desk. Shapes and notes dotted thick and thin lines across each page; it was a language she did not read. Her eyes casually followed up the wall behind them, where she paused on two very different frames hung beautifully; she felt uplifted at first glance and suspected that was their purpose.

The first frame was made out of twisted vines and gilded dried leaves hanging from their tendrils. Inside was a hand-scripted poem, written with flair and hand-dipped ink, which she recognized by the delicate droplets that stained the page. Embellished with images of cherubs, the page of prose was also flecked with gold. She melodically read it aloud:

<u>My Symphony</u>
To live content with small means.
To seek elegance rather than luxury,
and refinement rather than fashion.
To be worthy not respectable,
and wealthy not rich.
To study hard, think quietly, talk gently,
act frankly, to listen to stars, birds, babes,
and sages with open heart, to bear all cheerfully,
do all bravely, await occasions, hurry never.
In a word, to let the spiritual,
unbidden and unconscious,
grow up through the common.
This is to be my symphony.
~ William Henry Channing ~

Nodding in recognition of how good that felt to read, Stella understood why the poem was hung so graciously; it was a beautiful sentiment indeed. Music is time travel; it has the power to transport. Stella placed it like a pin in the fabric of time, often marking experiences she could return to with a single note of the moment's song. This unusually musical moment, oddly enough, was a silent one.

The other larger frame was simpler and looked to be made from thin slats of birch tree, recognizable by the white and speckled bark. The frame of carefully matched pieces of wood crisscrossed at the corners appeared to be secured by tiny thorns used as nails, and a large thorn to hang the frame from the wall with twine in a truly rustic fashion. It was cunning craftsmanship displaying natural beauty without the gold and flourish of the other. The two items side by side created a symmetry, the product of creative hands being guided by nature's offerings. It was both simple and spectacular.

The portrait itself was done on hand pressed flower paper, evident by the flicks of petals and greenery that wove in and out in a subtle fashion. The charcoal drawing was of a Conductor, *At last* she thought to herself, *this must be the occupant.*

Flowing lines and smudges showed a character in motion with a bowed head and hand pointing downwards. It read, "Reverberating deep joy," and with a sudden warmth in her belly, she knew what that meant.

Spiraling Up

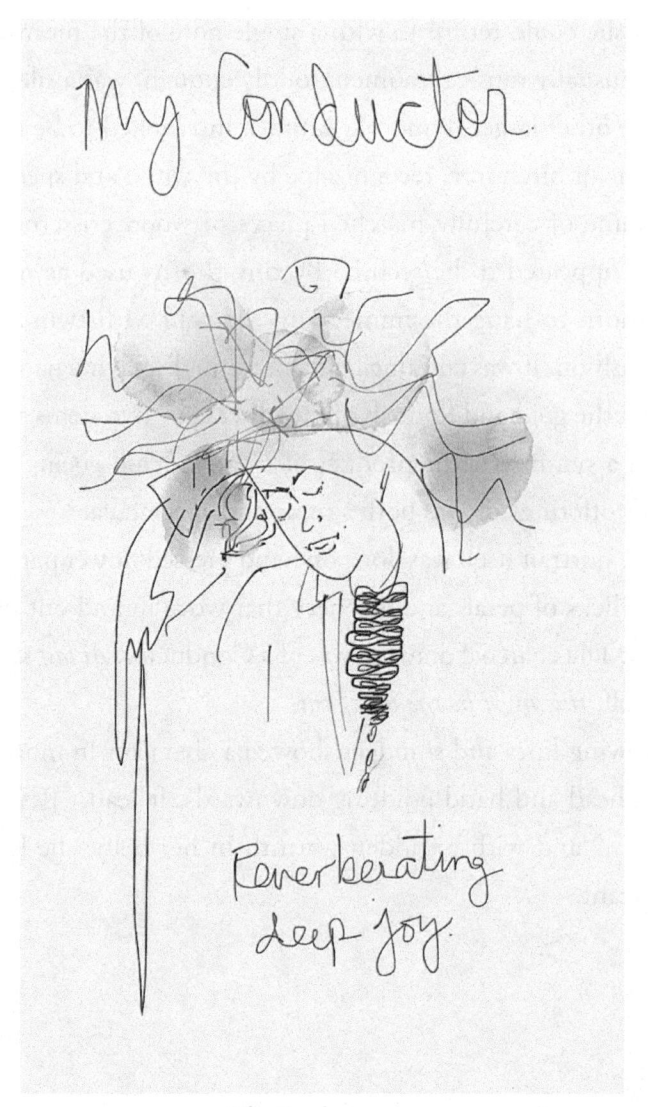

The Conductor

A glint of sun through a crack in the wall caught her eye and she followed it like a spotlight. There, glowing in a new light, was the instrument for a Conductor. It looked like a magic wand rising out of the hand of a tree. She took a moment to make sense of what she saw, and it was indeed a burled arm extending a knotted grasp that showcased and protected this object of great honor.

The grip of the baton, nested in the fist of burl, looked like a golden droplet, rounded for the palm. It was made of clear amber, the color of Serophant's eyes, and within the droplet frozen in time was an iridescent beetle resting like a crown jewel.

With closer examination, aided by the beam of light practically vibrating the colors within it, she realized the shaft was made of agate, a stone born of ancient wood, perhaps from the core of the very tree she stood within. It was two feet long and exquisite. Sparkling through variegated shades of creamy whites and browns, it radiated the creativity of the maker and the solemnity of the eons it took to reach its destiny and become the Conductor's baton. It took her breath away.

She became aware that her return here would be through her own symphony, and that the energy she could feel pulsing between her and the walls of this giving tree was the feeling of creation. "Whew," she said out loud shaking her head, "I hear that."

Unsure if she had been wandering this room for hours or minutes, she suddenly felt like it was time to go. With little else to catch her attention, and a notable sense of contentment, she let herself integrate the marvel of this tree-hut with a few deep breaths and wandered back outside.

Looking around from the doorway, she noticed a simple foot path down a slope towards what sounded like flowing water. Stella assumed she was near another bend of the river, and a stop there felt like it might be refreshing. Slowly making her way down the slope, she heard someone ahead of her and hoped it was the Conductor.

A few more steps and she could see her hopes had come true. At the edge of the rapids, there stood a tall figure with loose flowing hair, draping clothes and long limber arms. He held a simple stick in one hand, painting imaginary lines in the sky. There were no instruments.

Spiraling Up

There was no band, no song she could hear, and she couldn't help but feel she was missing something.

Standing back, she watched, careful not to disturb the silent performance. It was like watching a mime pretending to lead an orchestra. It wasn't long until the figure before her lowered their arms and head, as if taking a bow, and then stepped back from the podium. It was exhilarating to watch.

The next moment, they were locked eye to eye, and it was then that she heard the voice from the trail, deep and welcoming. "You found me!" Stella nodded with a smile and introduced herself.

"Stella, hello. I am the Conductor, a timeless soul creating the symphonies of life on the wind. I am but a guide to help you find your key. You have discovered some keys on this journey already, the Clearing Key and the Grounding Key, I believe. That is the path you took to get here, was it not? Now, I hope you will find your next key here, the one that will teach you to attune discernment so you may find your harmony. With it, you will begin to hear your own symphony."

He continued after a breath, "Follow this trail along the edge of where land and water meet. It is the riparian trail, where two opposing forces find their common ground and flourish with life." Confirming what he said, the Conductor pointed down the river. "Continue along the Open Heart Cascades through the Full Spectrum Stretch and you will find yourself at Hinterland Hall in time for the Sunset Symphony." He then pointed across the river to rows of bench-like seats tucked into the riverside greenery.

It was then that it clicked for Stella that she was standing at the pinnacle of it all, the place the Conductor conducts. This is where the music happened. She queried, "If this is your podium and that is the hall, where do the musicians sit?" "Musicians?" he sharply retorted, "Musicians listen to my symphonies to find inspiration for their own.

Much like you did earlier, they hear my symphony in the wind. I convene the rhythms, harmonies and melodies of nature's acoustics and exalt them with symphonic reverence to be heard by and guide those in need."

"The sounds of the bees, a rustling of leaves, birds that sing and the ting of a drop of water on a stone—this is my instrumental section. I guide them into alignment so they resonate stronger, farther and clearer with every note, every rhythm. There are infinite songs for infinite days and nights, yet they are only heard when listening. My symphonies are found in the stillness of one's soul, the quiet of calm and the awareness of everything and nothing all at once." Laughing, the Conductor finished with, "It's that easy!"

Deep down, Stella knew she had heard many such symphonies in the wind, on the shores of the ocean, in the stillness of a forest, in the silence of morning. She knew of what he spoke, but still her brain could not make sense of it. Regardless, with a sigh, she released the logic of it all and allowed it to be.

"Go on now, Stella. Follow my words and find your key. I have things to do that you have no part of," the Conductor asserted as he motioned down the trail, smiled with a gentle but firm nod and then turned back towards the podium to continue silently aligning the sounds of nature with harmonic intentions. With a grateful nod in return, she took the next step up a new path that wandered along a robust stretch of lush land and crystal-clear water lapping at the edge.

OPEN HEART CASCADES
The Place Where Land and Water Meet

Stella was replaying some of the Conductor's words: *Follow this trail where two opposing forces find their common ground, along the Open Heart Cascades and through the Full Spectrum Stretch, then you will find yourself...* She could not even begin to fathom what was in store for her next, besides another key.

Sure enough, the place where land and water met was just as it sounded—the edge of a river. It seemed like an ordinary water's edge, but she knew there was much to be discovered there. Her steps were slow, and her eyes were focused on both the big picture of beauty before her and the tiny insignificant things along the trail, as she had learned they could indeed be very significant.

She noticed a pattern emerging in the pebbles along the edge. They created a line too intentional to be natural, and she followed them to a hidden nook. She found an altar of sorts tucked into a nook of water lilies and a tower of sequentially smaller and smaller flat rocks rising from the shallows of the river. Upon the smallest at the top sat a sculpture of a woman holding a lily, gentle in features and wearing a flowing robe.

An etching on a big rock at the base said *Blessing to Kuan Yin for Divine Grace Where Land and Water Meet.* Next to that were several small rock stacks that seemed to mark a moment spent with her. Stella could hear Madam AuraCull's channeling of Kuan Yin in her mind, and she could feel a lightening in her heart with the recall. "Thank you," Stella said out loud with a nod. She spent a few moments with Kuan Yin's energy and then found a colorful stone to leave on the stack in gratitude before heading towards the main path again.

The river was flowing fast. It was so clear, she assumed it was cold, but when she paused to dip her fingers in, it was not. The temperature was a perfect balance between refreshing and comfortable. The idea of taking a dip began to supersede all others. Her present location was not conducive to such actions, so she decided when the time was right, she would indulge her temptations and jump in.

Feeling good, she focused on the fresh air and how a cool breeze balanced the heat of the sunshine as she headed towards a warm, sunny afternoon. Strolling along the river, she occasionally startled a resident bunny or a little bird in the brush. Sights and sounds came into new focus, and she started to commune with her surroundings as if she suddenly understood them. *Attuning discernment to find your harmony.*

Forces of water moved down the mountain, fed by a thousand sources unseen. It could rise or fall in any given moment without effort; the purpose of the river was simply to flow. These were the Rhythm Rapids—constant in that they were ever changing. Boulders rose above the surface and became shaped by the water. Their resistant edges transformed and became frictionless, smooth like velvet; they had succumbed to the constant pressure against them. The water's dynamic force offered Stella a new lesson.

There was a time Stella felt a force like that every day; pummeling against her, wearing her down, pressuring her to shape herself with no regard for her own will. Eventually, she was worn down, losing herself, immobilized and vulnerable to the pressures of people around her. Watching the forces in front of her collide, it called forth the pain and memories of backward days.

"Unlike the boulder, I can discern the forces that pound against me and choose what, if anything, I will change into. When external pressures can't be moved, then I can move myself." These words flowed like the river, steady and forceful. She was confident they would trickle down to where they needed to go so she may at last learn how not to repeat the hard stuff.

As if a flash flood had broken through, she was rewarded with a sense of validation. She was literally on the path to find herself and each of these moments helped integrate her lessons. Like each grain of sand builds a beach, each validation set her awareness in, creating the next from now, not then. "Now that's a shortcut," she registered.

Her awareness went into hyperdrive. She felt a warmth in her belly that began to spread up to her heart just as a spark of light danced on the water as if it was just for her, and a hawk simultaneously called out as it soared above; it was all in the key of YES. Validation, affirmation and awareness. "Wow," she said, "I feel capable."

What has actually changed, she wondered, *besides the way I feel?* In "real" life, the rock is still being pummeled by the water, nothing is different and a flicker of light doesn't change anything. Doubt had found its way into her revelations and strategically created dismay. The feel-goods were gone and a rush of cold overtook her. Just. Like. That.

With the immediate awareness of the contrast between her previously gleeful state and this one, she dared to question the weight logic should have in dictating her feelings at all. *Maybe feeling different is enough*, she considered. Aware she wouldn't choose to feel THIS way, and if all that had to change was her thoughts, then wasn't it better to simply choose to think better? "For sure it is," she muttered out loud in agreement with herself. "Think better, feel better." Flushed again with a positive charge, she ended her rambling thoughts with a *Reality Reset.*

Her connection to the signs around her was stronger, as was the inner dialogue challenging her interpretations. She had always felt a sense of deeper understanding, but now she was channeling in High-Def Stellavision—with brilliant colors and sharper images. She could see choices beyond giving in to that which did not serve her; be it thought or person. From where she stood, she could begin to see her challenges shifting to opportunities for exponential growth, fully embracing that every step mattered.

Would removing opposing tides create stagnant waters? Out of her head and into the world, her words were released "If not for the water, the rock would not take shape. A home for animals or a pocket for long-sought-after gold, the rock is not a victim of the water. It is an important contributor to the health and vitality of all that flows beyond it. And what does it do in response to the pounding? It smooths its rough edges, reduces friction and exposes inner beauty with luster as it's polished by each passing droplet."

She nodded in approval of this entirely new way to look at life, and it felt much better to imagine it that way. The fears weren't necessarily untrue, any more than the brighter perspective, yet the latter took a position of growth and contribution rather than defeat or retreat. The ability to discern harmony can simply be a matter of shifting one's perspective.

This shift brought on words that tapped into her brain like morse code: *You are the guiding star in your own tale. Follow the lessons that make you brighter. Awareness offers choice. Choose wisely.* The indelible message was received.

Both trails of thinking resonated in her belly, her heart, her bones; which felt right to her? Neither were wrong, but which allowed her to see insights that served her best outcomes? If she imagined the possibilities, did either spark an emotional response and, if so, was it desirable? *The questions activated her compass* like a spark within her spirit, pointing her to the path of elevated thoughts and rechargeable energy; think good, feel good, do good.

The contrast of feelings between these two thoughts helped her learn. A quick lesson to understand that her inner storyteller was the originator of the thoughts that drove her forward or kept her standing still. Being able to find the story that was the truest to her among all options, the one that aligned with her best self, was an intentional way to feel good…and feeling good is great.

Continuing along the steady, narrow path, she saw what looked like a bridge up ahead, leading her to the other side of the river. It was mostly hidden within the earth, like a stone iceberg. She could also hear intense water, like churning rapids. The Conductor did mention Open Heart Cascades; perhaps that meant she was nearing a waterfall.

The overpass turned out to be a wide rounded boulder that had been burrowed through by the river, creating a water tunnel and the effect of a stone bridge. Smaller rocks at either side were stacked as steppingstones, and after a few steps up, she was standing over the river.

The top of the boulder had been worn, perhaps by ancient floods and footsteps, into a flat wide walkable surface. Patches of moss clung to its edges and little nests of birds lived in the crevices, easily snagging tasty worms at the river's edge. As she crossed, she lingered and listened to the trickle of water flow beneath her.

While standing there, she could see ahead, and the Open Heart for which the cascades were named came into view. There was an exposed path carved into the side of the mountain, curving up and down a sloping side, then up and down again forming a heart shape that didn't

Spiraling Up

close to a point at the bottom. Within the center of the heart was an open prairie, dotted with wisps of motion and color.

Past the clearing was a wall of greenery shielding the cascading water with a bit of privacy. From behind it, a cloud of mist called to her like a blanket on a cool evening. She could feel her readiness, so she took a big breath of hope that she would soon be relaxing in the falls and stepped off the bridge up the path.

The heart-shaped path was not long or strenuous. It was lined with tiny flowers low along the grass. Petite daisies and violets, wild thyme and buttercups were scattered about and made her wonder if Lady JuJu had been there too. Around the bend and past the hedges, there it was: nature's shower. It had many levels, which gave it an unusual gentleness. Rather than a singular force falling from many stories, it was a short fall to a holding pond, then another small cascade to another pond and so on, until it poured into the large basin before her.

The edges were surrounded by rocks and plants, though a few spots had landings of soil to easily step in from. She found her way to a spot shining most brightly in the sun, which radiated a comforting heat. A quick test of the clear water told her it remained cool, though not uncomfortable. Stella opted to disrobe, everything but the magical key still around her neck; the thought of wet clothes was a firm NO.

She did not fear interruption or lack of safety, so she carefully undressed and piled her belongings in the sun. Slowly approaching the water, she stepped in. The interior of the pool was smooth, worn like those rocks in the river. Little pebbles thickly layered the bottom, perhaps ancient remnants of old boulders. They molded to her feet, creating a comforting and secure foothold that placed pressure on particular points like reflexology. Her body released hidden tension almost immediately.

Gradually, she walked through the swirling pool waist deep. The force of the waterfall was a bit destabilizing. She found the perfect spot to sit, shoulder deep and away from the cascade. She was part of the dynamic motion without the intensity of the push and pull. The mist created a drizzle effect, dampening her hair and landing on her face, similar to the feeling of the Faeries in the garden. She did a quick full dip, then relaxed as her fingers sifted through the pebbles at her feet.

She was always that girl on the beach playing with the rocks; this was a happy time and place she was gently being reminded of. With a fresh handful, she began to inspect them—color, pattern, size, shape. Though they were mostly tiny ordinary looking rocks, some jumped out as much more than that. Deep reds, pinks, purples, varying shades of black, even translucent ones, were present among the grays.

She knew rivers moved mountains, and that mountains grew gems, minerals and metals. It seemed this waterfall had become a bath of gems over time. Garnet, rose quartz, shungite, amethyst and quartz were but a few she recognized nestled in her hand.

She knew a few stones for their healing properties, something she had studied before. This was her first bath on this journey, and to be in waters charged with crystal energy in the afternoon sun was over the top—even for a land of magic. She closed her eyes, settled into the waters and let her mind and body float freely. She felt ethereal.

Her thoughts wandered to gratitude for the life she had. The life she was given. All these thoughts of trauma and pain that crept in were just a small piece of her story. She was so much more than all that. She knew, sitting in the waters, that when she walked onto this path, she left the self she knew behind.

Before this place, Stella carried a tiny glowing ball of self. She was in survival mode, so that light was as important as food, water and shelter. It was the catalyst that would propel her journey forward—the

Spiraling Up

core piece from which her truest self could grow. She used to hold onto the pain, loss, longing and trauma instead of her light, an act that delivered her to a dark place she didn't believe she belonged, allowing dark feelings to gnaw and nag at her as she drudged along wearing it all like an anchor.

Those feelings now felt muted, inoculated. The memories flashed in the present yet the energy behind them barely registered on her Richter scale of grief. She was floating into a new state of being. For a long while, her soul focus was how to survive, but in these waters, she was liberated. In this saturated aha moment, she learned how she could thrive moving forward.

She knew the source of her pains and how intense they could feel in her memories if she allowed it. But pain was not the only voice she had. She could find new stories, woven into the fabric of time, that she could retell to shape the portrayal of her experiences to one that felt honest, reflective and retold to shine her light.

She could see herself telling her story from her own viewpoint, her own voice, undisrupted by the recall, and it felt freeing! No one but her decided how she felt about the past and whether she sought resolution, honor or dismissed the narrative altogether; it was entirely up to her. She was evolving.

Undoubtedly inspired by being naked in a waterfall, the sense of liberty that washed over her felt like a reward for choices she has made. In the "real world," she often did things and did not always understand why. Here, she chose things based on how they felt and whether they charged that little ball of light within. Everything she was, she created.

She did not do this alone. This universal insight, her inner guidance and the tribe she loved at home all felt connected. Her choices had created the peaceful moment she was now enjoying: sitting in a blinged out bath of magic healing waters. "Yes, I created this!" In that declaration, she honored all her choices—"good" or "bad"—as each one had shaped her life and led her here.

Despite all the shoulds, musts, what ifs and disappointments, she knew in the deepest part of her spirit it was all meant to teach her what she needed to know. All the choices, the wins and the losses, the love and the heartbreaks, were worthy, if only for their role in her life as they all helped guide her.

She was not selfish or arrogant to claim her own world; she was empowered. Stella understood it was her destiny to embrace who she was and her soul power. She used to think this was easier said than done, whereas now she recognized that thought as a self-created barrier.

If she moved her feet forward, or not, it was her choice. Whether her stories highlighted her failures or strengths, she chose. "It's not egotistic or narcissistic to know that if not for me, this would not be. It simply is true, and so with that, I give thanks to me too!" Feeling vivacious, Stella splashed the waters high above her to shower herself with love.

She was glowing. She felt her chakras light up and beam from her as the water curtained over her, bridging the universal connection of earth, sun, water and spirit. It felt so good! Warm and tingly, she hollered, "It's a chakra-gasm!" giggling to herself while playing in the water.

Sitting in that pool, she was overcome with love for life and herself. Before this experience, she had been holding back the self-love and it created limitations—fear of not being good enough, embarrassing others or not rising to their expectations—that had too often stopped her from trying. Thinking to herself *May all paths that lead to those self-defeating thoughts melt away in these healing waters*, she said "RICH," aware of the release.

Then Stella exclaimed, "I want to live limitless! I am open to receive all that is needed to be as I am called for the greatest and highest good. RACE!" She paused for a deep breath and clarified, "I AM limitless!" *Yes, that feels better,* she thought. Then, she whispered, "I am enough." She was realizing she always had been.

With that, she washed the tears that had replaced the mist on her cheeks and cleansed her body with intention. "Everything I am, everything that is, shall be within my making. Please guide me to choose wisely. This is me, and I embrace my all. Reality Reset."

Still in the water recentering from that powerful stream of wisdom, Stella began to hum a song. A song to herself, full of love, for all of who she was. As it went along, it became stronger and deeper, turning into a serenade of love for all of her lives.

A deep baritone sound came out of her to reach her past, and a high soprano note sent love to the future. She was delivering the wisdom she had absorbed in this moment to be received by all versions of herself. Without comprehension, she understood that her soul self in all places and times now knew what she knew: this self-love and awareness was her birthright.

Her message became an incantation:

>Radiating love within me
>To whence I first began,
>Traveling through time and space,
>Healing all I can.
>Let the wisdoms of now guide me
>As I travel to and fro
>Enlightening every lifetime

So from this place we may grow.
RICH
As if by magic, let it be so.
RACE
Thank you, thank you, thank you.
Reality Reset.

And just like that, Stella snapped out of it. It took her a moment to realize she had gone into a sort of trance, present but not really. She guffawed as she thought this was the best bath ever! She felt like she had tossed a boulder of healing into her soul's pond and it was going to ripple for eons.

"What a profound experience. A bath that cleansed my lifetimes and washed them with my soul's infinite love and freed them with the ability to heal themselves? Yeah, okay, so *that* happened." At this point, she was having a full-on conversation with herself. Laughing at the moment, recognizing the cosmic awesomeness and embodiment of her deep connection to pure love, she felt expansive.

Before exiting the water, she picked out a rose quartz among the pebbles and decided to carry it with her. The pink healing stone was charged with the energy of love, so it seemed the perfect token. It wasn't to remember this unforgettable moment, but rather to be a beacon for placing herself back into the waters by simply holding it with intention. The stone would be a portal from anywhere to this healing bath under a blue sky.

Spiraling Up

Stepping out of the pool resonating an amazing sense of wonder, she stood in the sun a moment. When dry, she got dressed, put the new rock in her pocket, closed her eyes to acknowledge all the gifts she had received, then continued along the path.

FULL SPECTRUM STRETCH
The Prism Effect

A few steps down the way, Stella yelled out, "I feel amazing!" to the world beyond her. Her body, mind and spirit felt cleansed, renewed and recharged. It was clearly not just the muck of nature she had washed off; the deeper grit and old pain that rattled her thinking had also been washed away. They were not a burden to her any longer, and she was grateful for their absence.

She was recalling what the Conductor said as she left: "…through the Full Spectrum Stretch, you will find yourself at Hinterland Hall." She began to wonder if the "find yourself" wasn't so much a destination as it was a realization. Given how this journey had proceeded thus far, she was pretty sure there was still much more clarity to come.

Moving beyond the falls, she realized the mist still filled the air. Far above her, the falls started and went down hundreds of feet from where she was, each landing stirring up its own shower of fine mist. It seemed they all generously collected and hung in the air where she was with a density she hadn't experienced elsewhere. It wasn't quite a fog; it felt like infinite minuscule droplets suspended in the air that gently kissed her skin.

As soon as she focused her eyes ahead, she saw the Full Spectrum Stretch. She was walking in a prism, fully engulfed in a rainbow effect as the sun shone through the heavy mist. The water was everywhere, creating moist, rich soil and glazing lush fields. The scene was kaleidoscopic.

It didn't matter where she looked, or whether she was still or moving, pigments from all directions reflected on her skin. She felt enriched by it, soothed and inspired. She was already feeling great after her bath. She didn't think she could feel any better, yet here she was, elevating again. What was this feeling? How does good become great then become elated in just a few steps? Does one beget the other in a spiral up?

In that pause, she recalled how easy it was to slip from sadness to longing to despair, a much darker journey from her past. She knew how to spiral down quickly. *Why not spiral up just as quickly?* she thought. How did she not see this before? A warm sensation overcame her, and centering words poured into her heart:

> *Seek within to spiral up,*
> *Full spectrum vision is key*
> *To unlock depth perception*
> *And a colorful life for thee.*
> *A loving mind and open heart*
> *Generate your inner seeing.*
> *Share them often and abundantly*
> *To free your inner being.*

She wasn't really fazed by the otherworldly voice that had just filled her. Perhaps she was getting used to it? All she knew was that it felt good to hear. Its message resonated truth about the moment she was in. In poetic reflection, a tear ran down her cheek. Lifting her hand to it, the tear rolled onto her finger. It called in her attention, as if to say it encapsulated her wounded history. Simultaneously, she saw it too become a prism and embody its own full spectrum of color. This made Stella laugh out loud.

"Really? Come on…" she said with the kind of recognition one might get when they discover how a magic trick is performed. She continued to laugh through her words, staring at the teardrop still on her finger, seeing her memories captured in it and the radiant colors emanating out. She regrouped herself and let it be as it was.

Okay, she thought, *this is full spectrum vision.* "I see it," she said aloud, and with that, she whispered a little "Reality Reset," just in case. Within the tear, she saw a reflection of herself looking at herself fractalized to infinite smallness, and from there she saw color expanded out beyond the droplet's boundaries and surround her within a bigger sphere. Was she hovering?

As soon as she chose to let it be, she was suspended in a state of ephemeral bliss. She was aware yet disconnected, which she observed as a lovely state of consciousness. She was tingly and activated throughout her body, but it was internal. She felt no sense of her body's location in space, no sense of where the ground met her feet—if they did at all.

With nowhere to go and nothing to ponder, she was engulfed in waves of colored energy from feet to crown and then back down. Color pulsed around her and through her; it felt cellular. She felt like a glitter ball shaken up and all the tiny cells were dancing within her, sparkling and moving freely. Every part of her intuitively knew this was the feeling of infinite joy. It was the feeling of everything. She had tuned into the vibratory light of cosmic awareness. All she could think was: *This feels really good.*

She felt visceral energy all around her. Not the kind we expel or conserve, but in tingles and whispers skimming across her skin. She felt levitated, but she had no curiosity as to why, it just was, and it was okay to be that way. She knew the source of this energy flowed through every single thing on this planet. *It is the foundation of all we hear, see and feel.* Stella felt the embrace of the entire universe. She was one with it all.

When grief had consumed Stella, it made her forget her purpose and disabled her from painting the world with all her colors. This moment was showing her how she could create her life for new possibilities by learning what brought her joy and ignited her from within; by learning what made her shine in full spectrum. *I AM FULL SPECTRUM*, she thought to herself and with that she acknowledged her choices, her bountiful possibilities and the universal wisdoms that were making it all abundantly clear.

Not long before this fantastical adventure, she was learning how to breathe again; channeling healing energy, taking the time for focused reflection, and practicing mindfulness. Suspended in this moment, she believed she was experiencing a metamorphosis; through grief, through pain and into something wonderfully and uniquely her own. No longer feeling stuck in those deep feelings, she was now being offered a path through them. *This is life after death*, she thought.

Tracking what was happening was not why she was there, so instinctively she quieted her mind with acceptance and relaxed into the Full Spectrum Stretch, while color saturated her being. The synapses in her brain flashed connections like lightning, and she could feel her fascia flowing color to every part of her. She watched her breath become a fluid rainbow and felt it integrate into her blood and oxygenate her body. She was still, upright as if standing, and relaxed, but with a sense of buoyancy and forward movement.

Stella sensed a gentle nudge from her inner being, a reminder that all things must end. It eased her return to her body and consciousness and left her connected to the purpose of impermanence; it was part of

Full Spectrum Stretch

what made each and every experience unique and valuable. Stella had just made peace with the thought when POOF!—the bubble burst.

Hovering in Ephemeral Bliss

HINTERLAND HALL

A New Tune

The color Stella was enrobed in gradually faded to the ordinary, with the pace of a slow and steady exhale. She had no idea how long she was in her state of suspended color, but time no longer mattered to her after this invigorating experience. Moving forward and up became more important than ever, but at her own pace, and she was now ready for the next step. As she stood there looking around, she noticed the sign pointing to the trailhead of Hinterland Hall.

Before heading that way, she looked back but couldn't see much. The haze of the mist had created a veil that prevented her from viewing beyond where she stood. She couldn't recall seeing anything more than a stream of color before she felt a sensory overload. Hoping to prevent it from being a fleeting moment, she picked some nearby flowers in different colors and rubbed their petals onto a patch of cream-colored fabric on her pants to remind herself of what she was quickly forgetting.

It was a little discomforting to think she might not be able to recall the experience. This was the first time she was concerned that she was supposed to know something and had somehow missed it. Once she became aware that doubtful thoughts had started to gain momentum again, she chose to stop thinking about it, took a deep breath and checked in with herself to gather how she *felt* about it.

Spiraling Up

She knew immediately she retained all she needed to know. Positivity was flowing through her, and she felt compelled to generate more. There was no sense of loss, fear, trouble or worry; only the effervescence of pure bliss, vibrating through her in a connection to a source of energy greater than her own. She had no reason to entertain any thoughts that suggested otherwise.

To her, this was a feeling from a universal source of wisdom, compassion and possibility guiding her, a source known by many names. This connection was accessible to her at any time, offering abundant infinite love flowing through her entirety. Feeling complete, she stepped towards the sign pointing her way.

Hinterland Hall was marked by a small flag gently flipping back and forth on a tall post displaying a music symbol. She followed the narrow dirt path lined with dense shrub and brush, each one teaming with tiny birds hopping about, chirping a welcoming call.

The path opened to the clearing she had seen from across the river when she left the Conductor. Rows of chiseled, or perhaps gnawed, trees were lined up like benches facing the podium. The sun was descending past the edge of the mountain. It was not yet dusk, but the changing light seemed to announce the event would begin shortly.

Stella sat in the back row near the hedge away from others. She felt like witnessing the moment more than participating; she was still feeling lofty from her full spectrum stretch, a feeling she wanted to sit with quietly for a while.

She watched a few more attendees find their seats and get comfortable. There were also animals moving about as if to attend; beavers, raccoons, possums and squirrels all lined up along the river's edge facing across the water. Deer came in from the sides and lay on the open grass, and birds settled atop the brush alongside dragonflies and other various flutterbys. A carpet of light unrolled towards the podium's base and up the front edge where it stopped at the amber handle of the baton she saw on display in the treehut.

It made perfect sense to Stella, a gathering of Disney-esque proportions would occur at such a place. *Mystical, magical, wondrous* and *delightful* were all words that poured into her heart as her mind tried to find more ways to classify such a showing.

As the sky became pink with stripes of orange, it reflected across the river's surface and skipped along a stone path that narrowed from the river's edge up the other side. The baton was now standing tall on the podium, without the stand it was on before. With all the glory of the sunset, it began to glow up from the base, producing a thin line slowly reaching the peak and then a flash out of the top like a tiny supernova illuminated the Conductor who was standing behind it quietly observing.

Wildly present in stillness, the Conductor was now bathed in a golden light that quickly broadcast across the water, over all of the attendees and beyond, tuning them all in for the evening's symphony. While her eyes were fixed upon all that, Stella sensed movement on the bench beside her.

A bird blue and bold had landed next to her; at first glance she locked eyes with the bird and knew it was Serophant! It seemed he had shapeshifted to be with her in this dimension. His eyes were the same color as the light from the baton as he looked at her to say, "I'm so happy to share this with you." Before she could respond, their attention was pulled back towards the river as it seemed to slow down.

The turbulence had stopped. Where there had been rapids, there was now a gentle trickle and the quieting of it seemed to expose a new sound. Stella could feel a deep rumbling throughout when Serophant leaned in and said, "The mountain has arrived."

"Her springs are soothing us in a gentle tone, her soil is settling and her boulders are stretching their edges. Do you feel it?" "From head to toe," she whispered back, which gave them both a smile.

There were soft sounds of change as the contrasting dusky blues became the darkening shadows of the night. Was the mountain humming? The water began to act as an amplifier, boosting the broadcast's fullness to reach a visceral place. It was in that moment the Conductor picked up the baton, tapped the podium rim with it and lifted it towards the woodland canopy. With the gentle lowering and lifting of the Conductor's arm, the amber baton lit more intensely from within, creating a visual effect like a luminescent fountain pen writing poems in the night sky as the baton moved to and fro in a melodic rhythmic fashion.

The Conductor then pointed towards the river's edge and the frogs began to serenade everyone with a sweet song, lifting the listeners' spirits up to call in the night. Then, pointing to the brush nearby, small songbirds accompanied the frogs, all of it amped up by the water's resonance. With each point, a new instrument of nature was called in, stealing her attention. Stella was enveloped by the echoing symphony of tweets and twitters, the old school kind, the ones you only get offline.

The light of the baton then aimed at the trees all around, and on cue they began to rustle in the light breeze. Soft and tender, they shook and rattled with the symphony and their golden leaves reflected the light in a spectacle. The variety of sounds were robust and complex, and they were everywhere.

There was a bit of apprehension in the air as if nature had been waiting to be called in by the Conductor and become part of the full harmony of the Sunset Symphony. Eventually, all attendees became participants by the call of the Conductor's baton. A yellow light surrounded each being and pulsed uniquely to the beat of the heart within it—Stella included. With each beat, she settled into her connection to everything.

In a bit of a daze, her gaze landed back onto the Conductor, and she watched the mannerisms through soft light. A gentle fluid hand firmly held the baton as an extension of self, which quite clearly it was. Fabric from the shirt flounced and bounced along, moving in ways the all-but-motionless body didn't. Aside from the arm connected to the hand holding the baton, the Conductor remained still, nearly frozen. Both eyes remained closed, and the other arm seemed uninterested in all the commotion. It was relaxed off to the side and the Conductor's head leaned forward like an overheated flower.

There was movement in the shadows of the baton, which was hard to see at first, as the action became more and more intense. "I love this part," Serophant whispered to her while she watched closely to see what was happening. The whirl of activity around the Conductor began to create movement in the wildly strewn silver strands of hair, lifting it all as if defying gravity, yet she still could not see how. It was getting dark. The amber light of the baton still fell upon the Conductor, but it too was fading.

As the last of the light left the baton, the Conductor lit up again! Right on cue, lightning bugs sparked in a flurry of congruent spirals creating a stunning display. It was these fireflies that were creating a swirling wind lifting the Conductor's hair as they flew around the podium lining up for the show. She wondered if they might actually be Faeries spiraling in between and all around as the Conductor brought the audience to the crescendo of the evening concerto.

The baton pointed towards the water, and the river flooded in again and fish started jumping up and splashing about. Was one of them Fredrico? Then swiftly he pointed towards the woods like a call

Spiraling Up

to action and the forest joined in as owls with almost percussion-like hoots emerged from unseen perches.

It was now a full body expression. The ebb and flow of nature's sounds were being directed by a hand holding a wand away from slender shoulders with outstretched arms as wide as they could go. He now held his chin high, as if revived by the sounds he choraled. Then with a sudden flick of his arms, everything stopped. The swirling lights went dark, and the sounds in full resonance went quiet. She could only hear the breath of life.

In that berth of silence, his arms and head lowered to a natural stance, and slowly the Conductor's eyes opened to look at the audience for the first time. They were a brilliant blue that glowed from what she suspected was an inner light of his own; bright enough for her to see a contented smile on the Conductor's face as it turned to look downstream.

The baton moved once more and directly pointed to a pool at the water's edge with several loons casually floating in it. In that moment, they began to sing, or perhaps it was cry. Their song was an a capella serenade to the weary who saw the night as long and lonely.

There was a sadness in their song that paired well with the vacating light. A slight chill on a new breeze also accompanied the tune. It called in the evening air; cooler and sharper, making it a catalyst for transition. Stella felt it as an ode to all that was, an offering to all that is and a blessing for respite to rise and carry on once more. They were complex calls, vibrating in her belly, the space from which she summoned the strength to carry on. It was extraordinary.

When the loons finished as the sun disappeared, the only light remaining was the fireflies, once again swirling about the podium in harmony, drawing the audience's focus back. With a single final movement, the baton reached for the skies, and right on cue, the evening moon rose over the tree canopy. With that, the Conductor's arm came down and the symphony was complete.

The baton went back into its position on the podium and the Conductor's head fell to a bow as he stepped to the side and the fireflies casually flew away like scattering stardust. The crowd quietly applauded and honored the evening show with humble words of beauty and gratitude as they shuffled to their next destination.

Stella noticed the sounds one might expect were gently returning, unfettered and natural. The moon was shining bright overhead, and she saw the Conductor retreat to the cottage as the attendees began to move on. Stella looked at Serophant with wide eyes and wondrous joy at having experienced that. Tears were cascading over a huge smile and the only word she could mutter was "wow," over and over, quietly. Serophant set a wing on her hand and shared in the wonder.

Serophant asked her to follow him, and they hopped off the bench towards the brush on the other side of the clearing. As they walked through a dense area, he transformed back into his dragon self, or at least one version of it. He was about as tall as Stella, lumbering on all fours with wings tucked in tight and his long tail carefully rolled up in a curl like a chameleon's. They soon came to a smaller clearing where she found grass that had been laid over upon itself like a bed.

"This is for you," Serophant said, "The sun has set and it's time to rest. There will be more discoveries tomorrow. If it's alright with you, I will stay until sunrise and sleep beside you." Gushing with gratitude, Stella asked if she could have a dragon hug. As his arms stretched out, they opened wider than they looked and claws that were bigger than her head reached fully around her and lovingly pulled her towards his dragon heart, whose beat was as strong and comforting as the embrace. It was the biggest hug of her life.

Spiraling Up

"Thank you so much. Sometimes I just need a hug to remind me I am actually here. It's almost like it settles me into my own skin," Stella said. "Me too!" Serophant laughed, "Thanks for that, Stella. I feel better too." They warmly settled onto the ground, and Serophant offered a bit of his tail for a pillow. Cozy and comforted, they nestled in quickly.

"Serophant, can I ask you a question?"

"Of course," he mumbled.

"Today I traveled up and down the hills and valleys of emotions. I felt as joyful and elevated as ever, but just as quickly dropped back into some miserable feelings too. How is that possible? What does it mean to live a life of joy if it's so easy to slip back into dismal thoughts?" He sensed her trepidation and concern, knowing full well how fleeting the Full Spectrum Stretch is.

"Well, dear Starlight, it is possible because you are a being with free thought and great curiosity. Your mind wanders to many places. It is simply that you have not learned how to do it any other way. That is your journey." He repositioned a bit to lift a very sharp claw. "Let me share with you something MacA AyA and I love to ponder…" "You've met him too?" She interrupted. "Sure! You'll discover that beings of light and love tend to find each other on their paths through different lives," he said as the extended tip of a claw emerged and dipped into the moon as if it were an inkwell.

The stars were undisturbed as they became the background on his canvas in the sky. "This line is your horizon," he said as he drew a horizontal line, "It is where you rise and set from every day, the holding space from which all that you are stretches beyond. It marks your status quo, a foundation from which to ascend or descend."

"This," he said as he began to draw a line upward from the horizon into a series of rolling peaks and valleys that fell well below the horizon, "This line is your thoughts, your feelings, your flow as you live your day. Up and down, much of it is out of your control after all." Stella thought about the calls of duty and everyday life that she rode like a wave, or sometimes a roller coaster.

"No matter what I try, it's rarely easy," she quietly shared. "Hear me, Stella. Living in joy is not about removing the rise and fall that happens in life. Life is balance. It is harmony, it is yin and yang, it is golden symmetry. All that is on this planet exists to rise and fall. That is the course of life."

He continued, "When we fall, and choose to rise again, often we rise a little different, not quite what we were before. Like your journey through the Full Spectrum Stretch, you felt different afterwards. You shifted into something else without consciousness. Have you ever gone to bed feeling one way but when you woke you felt differently? Our soul's awareness can do amazing things when you get out of your own way.

"We can change in any moment, intentionally or not. You've seen me shift into different versions of myself, and I'm sure you thought it was unique! Believe me, Stella—you can shift yourself just as much within your physical form too, with the awareness that comes from an open reflection of one's own experiences. Looking back on the journey from a new perspective helps us find the lessons and carry forward from there."

"I just had a chance to feel that intense joy, Serophant, at the Open Heart Cascades. I felt the waters move the new awareness I have gained already on this journey through me and deliver it to all my lifetimes and selves so they knew them too. It was a wild feeling, and it felt true, sincere and deeply impactful. I really haven't left that cloud I rested on in that moment, though it too shifts in the breeze."

Spiraling Up

"Oh, what a perfect analogy!" Serophant said, then blew gently into the air to release his pictorial. He then pointed up, dipped in moonlight again and began to draw once more. "Now, in this space and time, this is your horizon." He drew another simple line and went on, "And you are on a cloud, rising and falling with the breeze, the shifts in your environment, and the terrain that you encounter." As he again drew a rise and fall to demonstrate the flow of life, there was one stark difference between this one and the first image: the ups and downs never dropped below the horizon line that marked her emotional well-being.

"You see, Stella, your feeling of elevation, the good stuff you carry, the cloud you ride, it still faces the same challenges of any given day, but you have learned one important key: to discern your actions within those challenges. You still have all of your emotions, but they never need to swing so far because you are grounded in a higher place, a more joyful center of self. You know it when you can find a way to be content with your own actions doing the things you do, especially the hard stuff."

"You face everyday things from a higher self, an inner calm and ease. You reserve dark spaces for when they are really needed, for there is no light without dark. You can never rid yourself of one or the other. Together they make you whole. Be warned, however, that they do not carry equal measure, for a pebble of darkness can balance a mountain of light. How you travel between these parts is up to you—that is choosing how to live your being."

"Is that manifesting?" she asked Serophant, "Feeding your desires to bring them to reality?" Nodding yes, he said, "Be careful what you focus your energy on or you may disrupt the balance. Do you know the magic to bring your focus from thought to a tangible life?" he inquired. "No, please share," she eagerly replied. "To manifest is to call something in with focused intention. You are energizing the possibilities through expression so they may become realities—helpful, destructive or otherwise."

Stella stared upon the new drawing, imagining that cloud rising and falling in her day, doing the same things that used to tip her scale with a new feeling. *I can create the life I want by holding my thoughts, words and actions above the fray of discontent.* "If it is that easy why aren't all people happy?" she said, seeking a reality check, while simultaneously recalling moments she knew she had experienced exactly what he described.

From concert tickets to sold out shows, to becoming the owner of her own business, there were dreams she could see with clear vision, feel as real as life and believed were so true they were destined to be. And those things did happen. On the flip side, the more she lived in fear, worry or anxiety and the more she focused on the worst-case scenario, the more she created that in her life too. When she fed her energy to the losses, she was feeding a wild animal. If done without regard, it could consume her! Energy is always voracious for more and eager to take whatever is offered, so she'd rather make it the good stuff. Being conscientious of what she was serving mattered.

This thought brought an image of FannySi to mind and how the ingredients she added were so much more than food. Stella suddenly understood she wanted to feed herself that way too. Serophant responded to her question, "For one, happy is quite different from joyful. It is a temporary emotion. It is an up that may follow, or proceed, the downs that are all part of life. Living joyfully is a place you choose to live from that is above the horizon line in the drawing. You can live a joyful life and still be sad or happy. It's as if joyful is the coin and those emotions are two sides of it."

Spiraling Up

Stella was intrigued as he continued. "A joyful life is a choice. It can take work to ascend to that place, and you are doing that work now, Stella. Many want to feel better but find themselves caught in a difficult loop, so focused on the problems that their spiral down keeps getting deeper. It's easy to do unintentionally. Cultivating only your desires takes practice, once you even realize you can."

"Even then, some people just don't want to feel better. Their identity is shaped by the negative, and they can choose to stay that way. They may never even realize they had options. And here's another tip." He wiggled his claw with a wink and said, "When beings show you who they are, believe them."

"Sometimes you need to create a safe pocket to allow yourself to feel okay. It gives you a place to start your spiral up. Like problems, good feelings can compound too, and the more you feel, the more they build upon themselves. That is how you find the tipping point that allows a shift to happen. It's a different path for everyone, but all paths start with the courage to take the first step."

"Thank you, Serophant, for helping me on my journey," she interjected. "Of course! To manifest the best of things, focus on the best of things and hold those outcomes in your vision. Outcomes, not steps! Focus on the end results you envision. Manifesting has three ingredients. Here's the secret," he said while playfully looking around and leaning in, *"Believe* in its truth, *know* it is real, and *feel* it happening. Belief is the lens, knowledge is a grounding rod and the feels are always a catalyst. EASY!" he finished with a robust guffaw.

Laughing along, she restated his words to integrate them into her awareness, *"Believe as if true, know as if real, feel it happen,"* and sighed, "Oh wow, I can feel that run through me!" Serophant chimed in, "Yes! That is the charge, the spark of propulsion that radiates out and attracts the very things you seek; intentional or not. Can you see why it's easy to harness the worst things too? Our intentions guide our focus, which drives our actions. I keep saying it because it is worth taking time, at any time, to be clear about your intentions as you proceed in life.

"Manifestation alone does not assure the path. This is why you must focus on the goal and not the process. If you have steps you desire, then manifest those as their own goals. If you are tethered to the process or timeline, you may get so frustrated by the way it all unfolds that you become your own barrier.

"Often many other paths must be crossed that you do not see or won't see until you turn around because you've gone too far. Other times yet again you may find a path leads you to never-imagined things and your desires change entirely. Desires for change can lead to changed desires, which is why you are guided to listen to your soul self and allow your evolution to unfold." Stella sat with that insight quietly for a moment.

After an extended pause, he blew the drawings away into the night sky. Stella was taking in all she could, allowing it to settle into her body and find a comfortable place to land. It felt like finding a missing piece to a lifelong puzzle; she somehow knew it was around, she was glad to find it and knew it was necessary to complete the big picture. Stella felt nurtured by the gentle manner in which this kindly blue beast shared his ancient wisdom.

Serophant continued, "Believing activates the heart, knowing activates the crown and your feelings activate your soul's desires." Watching him, she saw his eyes spark with an inner fire and a mischievous smile appear. "Then, when all is aligned with your inner light…" he stopped speaking and quickly pointed his talon to the sky to flick a comet-like explosion into a nebula of color hovering above her. "You have become the generator of your own destiny." Looking satisfied with his grand display, Serophant lay down next to her in the grass again.

Stella sank into her nest and stared upon the cosmos he had created. She uncontrollably yawned, to which he did too. Her lungs were expanding beyond themselves to breathe in the magic bestowed upon her. She had no words, just a hushed *wow* for the display she was witnessing. She simply accepted it and absorbed it all in through every pore, as her brain alone could not contain its entirety.

In that moment, Stella felt she was learning to be a counterbalance to uninvited pain. What a concept! As a contrast to the dark feelings and in discerning her thoughts towards what she wanted, her positively charged energy compounded and her cloud lifted. "Ahhh," she sighed to Serophant with a sense of contentment that soothed her deeply, "Good begets good."

She knew some days would be harder than others, but in this moment, she imagined herself being able to feel better when she did stuff that gnawed away at her, to hold her thoughts in a place that felt good even when doing tasks that didn't. *ESPECIALLY when doing tasks that don't!* she corrected herself. *I'll just ride my cloud*, now imagining doing laundry or dishes on a cloud. Could she break the drudgery with a silly visualization like that?

Yes—that was her answer; burdens could be lighter with a little levity such as that. Stella could see it was a way to strengthen the skill of shifting her nagging thoughts to something that didn't drag her down. If she could fill the mental void with thoughts that made her feel good, she would be creating her own symphony. She imagined that the best moments to come might someday remind her of this one. She was starting to believe that it's not how you do things, rather, it's who you are when you do them.

"Thank you, Serophant. I love you."

"I love you too, dearest Stella. Wake well." Then Serophant curled up beside her and left his hanging vision for her to rest her eyes upon as she drifted. In no time at all, she was asleep.

THE GENERATOR KEY

Energize the Possibilities Through Expression

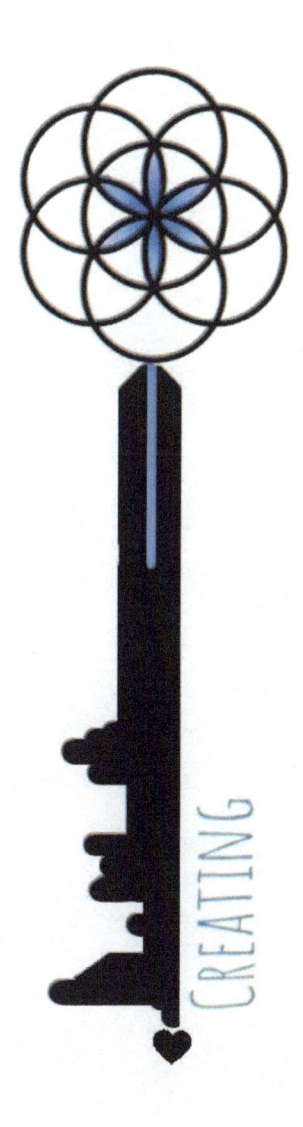

CREATING

FALLING-UP HILL
The Wisdoms of an Echo

The sun began to shine upon her sleeping in the brush. The warmth more than the light was what eased her awake as it quickly lifted the cool touch of morning. She stretched and cooed and said good morning to Serophant before she opened her eyes and realized she was alone.

She sat up, peeled back the field blanket and was greeted by a slip of wood with a pile of berries and nuts, an apple and a hard-cooked egg presented on a log now sitting where Serophant had been. She stood up and stretched a bit while enjoying her breakfast immensely, saying a thank you for the kindness and generosity. She lifted another acorn of sweet nectar as a toast, tossed it back and quenched both her thirst and sweet tooth.

She didn't linger long and decided to stop by the river and refresh herself. After a quick rinse in the gentle current, she headed up to the main path and began her day's steps forward. She felt a quiet ease about the morning like she was still on that cloud, though she was not flying high; she was feeling rather grounded, reset and calm. It was then that she realized she wasn't just ready for an adventure; today she was excited about what she was going to learn about herself and the world around her. She felt just right.

"Awareness is a full body experience!" She laughed, beginning to understand what came from the tiniest shift in her thoughts, her heartbeat and even the whisper of the wind across her skin. *It is worth giving at least a moment's focus to things that call my attention.* She was learning to trust that the messages she needed to hear were the ones she ultimately would focus on; she didn't need to worry about what she didn't know.

She was aware that the resonance that had settled into her core felt stable and confident after the amazing night's respite and attunement. In this fantastical reality, every step since she discovered the gates to enter this place were guiding her awareness and understanding of how she worked in the world. It was teaching her how to open herself to the input along her path and discern what led to the good stuff…and even what the good stuff was.

This morning, the path she walked up was straight and long. It was fringed by the occasional grassy flourish that sprung out of the gravel path. A small stream flowing down, perhaps a source for the Open Heart Cascade, accompanied the morning birds in song. The melody could have been from a sunrise show by the Conductor, and she wondered if she had slept through one.

Something came into view and she stopped, stared, then began again towards what appeared to be a boulder about the size of her home back in the real world, but it was shaped like a giant broken gumball. Its size was matched by a nearby tree that seemed to sparkle in the sunlight.

She could tell the boulder wasn't solid, but it wasn't hollow either. It was cracked and missing chunks, which created openings that a soft blue light was emanating from. There was life around it, on it, in it. She was heading right towards this epic sight and was intrigued to learn more.

She walked for a stretch, then sat in a small patch of wild strawberries nestled along the stream's edge to take a break. This was a steady walk, no push or pull, no pressure and she was taking it leisurely. Returning to the path, she continued for what felt like half the day. She hadn't even encountered the next patch of grass she saw so long ago, a patch she thought was just up the way.

"What is happening here?" she outwardly queried. By the time she encountered the next blades of green, the perceived small patch was taller than she. The boulder ahead was also far larger than she thought—it was the size of a city block! The soft glow seemed brighter too, and she began to sense a flow of energy swirling around her that wasn't there before. It was tingly, like a tickle. She acknowledged the pleasure in the moment with a big smile and a quiet thank you and walked on up the path.

Further still, she walked for what felt like another half a day, yet the sun never passed her; in fact, it still sat quite high above. Her perception of time was lost in this place. Each step forward felt a bit like she was on a treadmill.

Stella started to let her mind use the time to ask questions of herself to see if her curiosity could find an answer. What was this strange idiosyncrasy opening her eyes to?

Am I spending time moving forward without feeling like I am really accomplishing anything? Am I focusing ahead with expectations rather than allowing it to unfold?

"The first thing I thought of when I saw it was home." With a sigh and a thump in her heart, she answered herself for a full circle conversation. It wasn't about missing home; rather, her mind led her promptly down another wandering path from that place. "My home is broken too," she said with sadness. She decided to sit at the edge of the creek again and ponder this for a little longer.

Her hands ran through the pebbles on the ground. She wondered if any of them were once as big as the glowing orb, or perhaps they were pieces of it scattered about in little bits over time. She knew that feeling. *UGH!* she thought, *Why this? Why now? Why do I shift so quickly?*

It was a deep and heavy feeling of old pain that swept over her the instant she had that image of being broken and spread about. She was frustrated with her reaction and desperately wanted to be done triggering this way. She quickly identified the source of it, another sign of her evolution, and with that awareness she felt a premonition about what was coming next. She knew that this was *that* part of her journey. She had arrived at a place to help her release the tethers that bound her emotions to memories.

"Wasn't it just last night I learned how to reharmonize my thoughts? I can recall a story without crippling pain from memories. I want others to know me authentically and I want to share what makes me…me. I was broken…" she said in annoyance, then paused for a reflective breath. She recentered and restated with emphatic clarity to mark her place in the present, "Now I am whole."

Surprised at how she had caught her words and redirected them, she sat a moment longer to appreciate how far she'd come already. After all, it was not something she would have thought to do before. With renewed gratitude, she rose to make her way once again up the perpetual path, whispering, "Reality Reset."

Practicing the skills Serophant was teaching her last night, she spent the next bit of path calling in the cloud she was riding on earlier. She imagined it back underneath her feet. She was nearly there.

Stella no longer had a reference for the massive size of the giant sphere as she stood in front of it at full scale. It was not a boulder; it was a ginormous geode— a jagged, round, broken stone exposing its brilliant internal pellucid world. If it had been underground, it might have been called a crystal cave, but this was above ground, resting in the sun, perfectly imperfect, which was only part of what made it beautiful.

Falling-Up Hill

Her path led directly into the glowing and vibrant stone, but before going in, she decided to wander around and savor the timelessness of the present. She knew it was okay to take her time; she was not in a rush. The beauty of all around her was for her to experience, discover, connect with; but mostly, it was so sparkly she wanted to see more!

From the trail leading inside, she pivoted towards the tree that hovered over a nearby grassy shaded area. There were flower beds growing in the shade of the tree on trailing vines that flowed down the geode's exterior walls, creating falls of bouquet curtains in whites and pinks. When they reached the soil, they burst into small pastures of blooms among the grass.

The giant tree grew through the broken edges. It had integrated itself with the geode, stretching branches through any crevice it could, creating a stunning mosaic effect. Stella stood beneath it and could only reach her arms around a quarter of the trunk. When she did, she felt a pulsing that made her linger. It synced with her heartbeat, and her resonance was amplified through it. The tree was a beacon, expanding her energy into the soil through the roots and back up to the sky through its crown.

She let go and felt really good. Stepping back beyond the canopy, she could see crystalline dust all the way up the tree, which seemed to be accumulated over eons, sparkling in the sun like Tiffany's diamonds.

Stella wandered back towards the path, then past it and around the other bend. She walked the trail for a few minutes, and it wound through some shrubs and brush along the base of the geode. It stopped soon after at the edge of a cliff. Leaning forward, she definitively said NOPE and backed up quickly, turning towards the entry to her next adventure.

Like a ball that sits on the ground, the base was narrower than the middle, but it went deep, so the passage was recessed below ground level. The path ended at a few-foot drop; sudden though not very far down it was nothing compared to the cliff she had just seen. From there, it curved back up on a steep slope toward another ledge well beyond her reach above. Its shape and purpose made no logical sense to her, but this was where the path led, so she knew she needed to proceed somehow. She wasn't sure how she would do it, but the only way forward was down.

She wrung her hands together while reminding herself to keep grounded, both literally and spiritually. "WATCH YOUR STEP!" she warned herself firmly. She was now choosing to go far out of her comfort zone and needed to be okay with it. A few breaths later she took a step.

"NOOOO...". Immediately, she slipped and plummeted, screaming as she panicked and clambered to grab something—anything—to catch her fall. Besides forgetting it was only a few feet down—a death-defying stunt this was not—in her state of panic and fear, she also didn't notice she was falling UP!

A moment later, she landed with a thud on the ledge that was previously above her. Searching for breath, trying to calm herself, she sternly said, "What a way to start!" She rolled over and clung to the roots of nearby brush as she peered back over the edge and saw the place she was standing a minute before.

Scooching away from the ledge and onto her back again, she closed her eyes and focused on relaxing. The first step was to slow her breath. It wasn't necessary to understand what just happened in this moment; she simply needed to know she was safe, and she was.

In her hand, she gripped a fist full of roots from a nearby bush as a tingle of a message from within began. She allowed herself a moment to recall what she had recently learned and the Ancient Grandmother's wisdom began to come through:

> Grounded, aligned and open,
> Breathe my essence in.
> From root to crown
> And then back down,
> My clearing now begins.

Just like that, she was back in her body, her mind was calming and her fist unclenched. In utter confusion of the last few moments, she remained supine and reflected on her state of instant fear. The unexpected and uncontrollable suddenly plunged her into an unfamiliar panic. She had an overwhelming sense that she was about to walk a path of letting go of assumptions and control to guide her to be present instead of reactive.

She did not want to step forward in fear, and she sensed this part would not be easy; she lacked confidence in what had happened or would happen. Lying there, she began to see the assumptions that had caught her off guard that day. From the short path that took all day to walk, to falling upwards, the ordinary was not so in this place.

Her distorted perspective of distance and time altered her experience in a way that placed her ahead in the outcomes instead of present in the journey. When the outcomes felt unreachable, she began a spiral of frustration.

That irritated thought pattern bridged to memories of misdirection that would come at her from some of the people in her world, in her home. Losing her footing and feeling out of control threw open a door in her psyche, and the yucky stuff came flying in. She realized she may have landed in a mild panic attack as she intentionally focused on calm. "Each breath helps me reset."

Her mind continued to wander as her breathing steadied her. "We all need a neutral place to be. A place that neither pushes nor pulls, encourages nor defeats. A library-like place, quiet and still, within our body. We are a torus of energy, and within the donut of it all is a space, neutral and simply present, even if a tornado of detraction surrounds it. It is like yin and yang; one does not exist without the other. A hurricane must have a calm center to be a hurricane."

Neutrality was a place Stella discovered within when she fell into deep grief after loss. Lying there, she found a space within that was not serving its purpose. Her neutral place had been mistaken for a holding place for all the "when the time is right" conversations that never happened. Some day she would get to share these thoughts and pains, needs and dreams with her loved ones, when the time was right for them. These parts of her were left in limbo; crude and unfulfilled. A self denied was set aside to tend to the priorities of others.

Amongst the wreckage of pain, she also found some dreams kept safe from others. Imaginings of what could be were hiding in the core of her spirit. She needed to sort them all and decide their fate one by one, as if clearing a pile of leaves individually.

She sorted them out without lingering on them first. Some were easy to decide and move through. She would keep a few because they were too beautiful not to and discard what did not serve a purpose to become composted soil that supported future life. That painted a picture in her mind that felt good and helped her bloom in her own garden; a thought that brought a smile back to her face.

That left a pile of the wettest leaves, the sticky, rotting, mashed together leaves, waiting for her to dive in. She decided it was too much in the moment and set them aside, again, for another time. She bagged them up for another day.

Underneath it all she found a softly glowing pebble and immediately knew it was the little ball of light she had been nurturing. *Is this what the Conductor meant by "find yourself?"* Stella lifted it up and cradled it in her heart where she could feel it nestle into its new home, promising herself she would never let it be buried again.

When she did, it began severing the burdens of others by untethering their hold from her body, mind and spirit. *Snip –snip*. The strings were cut, and like a newly freed balloon, she felt a sense of being lifted. She sighed to herself, "Things are looking up."

"UP!" echoed in response along with a big boom above, like the crack of lightning. As she glanced up, a broken tree limb fell through an opening in the geode. Falling without risk to her, it landed up the path a bit. The pale bark then unfurled itself from the branch like a scroll offering itself to her. Another small branch nearby was standing upright in a dark pool of mud like a quill in an inkwell. In a flash she could see her next moment come to life.

Stella gathered the offerings and found the flattest piece of earth nearby, unscrolled the paper-like bark and wrote a letter to the dead. She realized she had to open that bag of leaves up and let the contents go. Taking the healing tools offered, she proceeded to free her soul.

Her words were filled with pain and sorrow and loss, feelings left to decay within when widowed. Her ability to store was vast, and she was shocked by the volume of unresolved issues she had held onto and allowed to remain buried. As she wrote, the emotional clutter seemed huge and dramatic. It was astonishing to think she had experienced it all, yet the one thing that hurt the most was none of that.

It was a single word used as a weapon to diminish her worth over and over again. She said the word out loud, "Whatever," with the usually accompanied shrug. A diminishing word that became a blade that cut her down to a mere sliver of her authentic self; in this moment she was learning to separate herself from the oppression.

She knew she had to let go of these triggered memories, and doing so required her to be okay with leaving things as they were, unfinished.

It was hard accepting some things would remain unresolved; like all she never got to say, or hear. There could be no more longing for such things if this moment of release was to be complete; she was ready. It had to be okay for it to be as it was, a feat of mercy and grace for herself—and others.

A creature of clarity and awareness, Stella yearned to KNOW things. KNOW people. KNOW truth. Yearning, however, has its own pain. Yearning for something you cannot get, such as resolution with someone who has died, is a powerful force. She knew the weight of sorrow when one yearns for what they cannot have. Growth requires one to accept that the answers are not needed to carry on. It is important to acknowledge that some things are simply not meant to be known and to trust that what is already known is what's important.

After huge loss, it took a breakdown for her to begin to recover. She fell down a bottomless well of despair, or so she thought, until she listened to the channeled wisdom of Abraham Hicks speaking of yearning. The message was an external relay of her internal wisdom, everything she heard, she knew, but she needed to listen over and over until she could feel it, believe it and fully integrate it into her consciousness.

It was ten lonely, desperate grieving days before she believed: *There is nothing lost in what was had. It is always with you.* The longing for what can be no more is fear of what's to be instead. If she remained honest and loving to herself, fearless of the possibilities, she would discover in time what was meant to be.

She nodded in validation with a deep breath in of the awareness that rippled through her. She felt a new heat rise from within; it felt like love for herself, and its source was the new heart light she had successfully rehomed. Her breath became smokey as it rose from her lips. She smiled with a little sass, and with a burst of inner strength,

Spiraling Up

she exhaled, "I'm on fire!" and she watched her words land on the bark. They sparked! Quickly the embers consumed the corners and then burst her documented pain into flames.

She heard a distant word come back to her, "Fire," and just like that, the pages were ash on the ground. She then watched her thoughts shift, becoming climbing gear to scale the narrow walls of grief she had once occupied. *I am what I think I am.*

"Well, I AM going to watch my step," she giggled as she stood, preparing to walk again. *Perspective, neutrality, release*—these were the words jumping out at her, so she called for clarity and connection to the energy around her. She was answered with a sense of assuredness. That was enough for her. She nodded her head in gratitude and then heard a loud and final word within: *WITNESS*.

She felt well enough to proceed. Gathering herself back up, Stella channeled her calm, collective strength into a vertical position. She moved awkwardly to stretch her body and mind, reaching high above her head, then as low as she could go, allowing her muscles to stretch and loosen, finding a fluid and relaxed place to settle into for the mysterious path ahead.

The space she had landed on was a modest ledge, rounded like a period at the end of a sentence. Only a narrow trail leading into the geode offered forward momentum, though all she could see of it was colored light brightening the other end of a stone tunnel she was about to walk through. Inside it, the arch was tall and slender with ragged edges. It felt as though it narrowed more and more as she proceeded. When she popped out the other side, she was relieved to be there.

The word *witness* began tossing around in her mind like clothes in a dryer. It was a word she knew well enough, but it felt like a challenge. *How odd*, she thought. In its simplest terms, she was being guided to observe what was around her without interaction, and she was noticing a visceral response to the idea.

In an attempt to get her bearings, she listened to the advice and slowly evaluated her surroundings, looking for details and signs of next. What she witnessed took her breath away. The hues of the sky seemed to be captured in the crystal structures that created the landscape of this inner world. Each surface was mineral, stacked, grown, cracked and aged for millennia. The color, however, was not reflecting on the surface of the quartz; it was within, emanating the blue glow she saw upon first sight.

The surfaces varied from slick, slabbed and striated to what could be stairs and ledges, cliffs and turns. She also noticed patches of dense and less colorful stones that seemed to grow where one might need extra footing as their rough edges created a gripping surface. "Okay," Stella thought, "that seems to have a lot of intention and purpose. Perhaps there is much more to see than what I simply look at."

She noticed she was emotionally charged by the idea that being witness was foreign to her. Despite the offending accusations by her own mind, she found the need to follow them into an internal dialogue and chip away at the truth of her reaction. Almost defensively, she exclaimed, "I'm a leader! As a leader, I observe, of course, but I am not a spectator. I am a catalyst, a creator, a doer." All these things she was proud to know about herself.

"Witness, participate, lead, follow—I can do it all!" she confidently declared to herself. "So, why does the idea of being a witness make me feel intimidated?" she wondered. A quick answer came like the snap of a finger: As merely a witness to a moment, she had no voice, no hand, no input of any kind. Period.

"So, it's about control..."

Stella knew her triggers: feeling stepped over, minimized, voiceless. The idea that she had no say in her world was crippling, and holding on to her voice was something she deemed worth fighting for. The power struggles with loved ones' expectations pulled against Stella's need to simply be who she was, and it created a deep wound she hoped may now at last heal. The echo of old words still cut deep and revived painful scars.

"That's not the whole truth though," she called herself out, "A witness is not powerless to affect a situation, even if they aren't in control." She continued to converse with herself to find her truth. Why did she feel that so strongly? Where is the power of a witness, she wondered, if not with interaction or communication?

To witness is to observe, catalog, identify and surrender. A witness in its purest form is a record of a moment in time beyond the self. Bird watchers, journalists, scientists, artists all witness acts around them with the intention to allow them to unfold as they will. The act of witnessing, in fact, is a catalyst for participation; if what is observed is shared, then action has already been taken. This is a validation that something has occurred—but ironically the perspective is often different from that of others who have witnessed the same thing.

"We stand alone in a singular perspective of anything we see," she said with a beaming smile, alone, in a giant geode. Without thought, she howled a "HELLLLOOO!" to which she heard back, "Hello," though it seemed a little different from how she had said it.

She continued with slow footsteps along the narrow trail. The only thing going fast was her mind. There was brilliant flora and fauna which cascaded in and over crooks and crevices to reach for the beams of golden sunlight that pierced through from the outside in contrast to the hues of blue within.

A bit up the trail, Stella was at her first crossroad. She encountered a choice of directions. The one she was on continued, steady and transparent. Another veered off to an upward slope beneath quartz stalactites, and yet another was unknown as it led into a pitch-black cave. "Which way should I go?" she said out loud sarcastically—to her there was only one choice.

In return, she heard a resounding, "Go!" *Another echo?* she wondered. It came with a sense of pressure that she had neither expressed nor appreciated. Upon examining her choices, she felt a strong gut reaction that said NO to the cave. The other path was, for lack of a better word, neutral. *Could it be that easy?* "Sure!" she said, "Let it be that simple." With a grateful nod, she followed the feeling of YES and carried up the path she was already on, then she heard the word "simple" come back her way.

While pausing in one of those moments, she released the sense of pressure she felt a minute ago and sought the perspective most beneficial instead. She allowed herself to be open to and aware of whatever she needed to witness. She did not need to keep emotionally diving deep either. "Stay present," she reminded herself.

"Perspective, neutrality, release, witness…basically keep my cool," she mumbled to herself on repeat as she gingerly walked. She focused on those filters while she carried forward on the path, checking in when new options presented themselves. This happened repeatedly, and Stella was starting to notice what a YES and NO felt like. She discovered she knew them much quicker in her belly than her brain. "I will follow the yes!" she whooped along with Madam AuraCull in her mind. Her exclamation was followed by a distant "yes" in reply.

Feeling more confident with every step, and possible misstep, she started to look up from her feet and really connect with the incredible place she found herself. She looked out into an Escher-like inner

Spiraling Up

world. It was vast and complex. A jumble of steep ledges and sharp edges curved up, down and all around. But the more she looked, the less chaotic it became. It was the golden ratio, and with that thought, her vision shifted and suddenly she could see the geometric pattern repeating in clusters large and small all around her.

The top of the dome was broken open like an egg, and the cascading tendrils of flora hung high above her like living chandeliers. The blue light she had seen beaming outward now fully encompassed the space. It was not from a singular source; the light pulsated throughout as if the geode was breathing the colors in and out, becoming lighter and darker, swirling in rhythmic patterns deep within each facet of crystal. It was everywhere—and circulating within the geode itself.

She did not see any animals, not even a bird flying within the sphere, despite the many crags and openings that allowed for ample nesting spaces. Actually, there was no sound either. No bird song, no wind, though the air was not stagnant. Instead of complete silence, there was a sort of white noise emanating from everywhere. *Or should I say, "blue noise?"* she thought, feeling witty, given the dominant hues.

The limited spectrum of colors and sounds helped her stay rooted in the present, observant and feeling relaxed. The sounds were calming, and the colors eased her mind too. She recalled the chakral blues; azure blue representing the throat, and deeper tones of indigo representing the third eye.

A new tingle in her belly promptly reported back she was onto something. She let her mind follow that energetic nod of awareness. *The throat chakra helps us resonate with external sounds to allow our own communication from within. This helps us find that deeper truth of self and express it with clarity.*

"That's a yes," she spoke out, which was distantly followed by a "yes" in reply. While thinking about her third eye and tuning into the deep tones of indigo and wild berry pulsating through her surroundings, she saw a pattern she hadn't noticed before. The color fluctuations were not haphazard after all; rather, they were a sequence of colors, seemingly chasing each other in a playful swirling dance.

The third eye chakra is centered in the forehead and helps connect us to our intuition and perceptions of what's ahead. When aligned and attuned, it helps us see the wisdoms of the past and guide them through the present and beyond. "Awareness is a funny thing," she mumbled, "you can't unknow what you know."

"Was that an AHA?" she asked herself jokingly, only to hear an "AHA!" in a bit more of an exuberant tone bouncing back at her. Curiosity about the echo was coming to the forefront. She felt an inner answer: *An echo is a chance to reflect on a moment for a moment. Reflection offers perspective, clarity and the ability to rECHOose another course.* "Clever," she said to herself, which was then corroborated with a "clever" in return, giving Stella a big smile and a small laugh.

With one step in front of the other, she walked her topsy-turvy, crystalline path and started to focus on the sounds she heard again. They were deep and gentle yet somehow larger than life—a rumbling, guttural distant thunder. It was deeply soothing, and a sense of contentment washed over her. She felt embraced.

Breathing softly, walking easily, she began to feel she was moving as one with a swirling dynamic energy—no longer a witness. She realized how she felt about things was the filter she projected her perception through. Whatever it may be, the core of her being illuminated all she was, much like the inner workings of the luminescent geode.

She walked up to a sheer perfect piece of crystal reflecting her image back at her. Responding to the moment, she declared, "I am my own echo!" to which she heard a "yes" in return. "Wait, what?!? That's not what I said! Who are you?" In a distant reply, all she heard was a simple "you." Stella let out a guffaw, shaking her head. She did a face palm while thinking to herself, "Of course you are, of course, of course," through laughter.

The foliage was hanging and looping around the mirror. She noticed a single crystal that appeared to have grown within the plant, and it immediately drew her in. Reaching for it, she realized it was not connected to a larger structure; it was caught up on a snag and dried, perhaps broken in a storm and left to sit until she came along. It was a perfect circle of twisted vine, braided in many layers around a shard of crystal, singularly flowing with its own display of blue-violet optics.

The Crown

Stella instinctually placed the crown-like find on her head. WOOSH! Once again, a rush of energy and insight flooded in. Lifting her gaze back to her reflection, she saw the crystal sitting directly on her third eye and it fit her perfectly—too perfectly. She decided that this was not likely a fallen branch from storms long ago but rather another incredible gift. It was hanging next to a mirror after all!

This was the gift of focus. The stone started pulsing with bluish purple light and opened a portal in her third eye. Seeing clearly, she could intentionally energize her best possibilities through expression and learn to create what she desired in this life.

The word *manifest* had now taken up space in her mind, pouring through it like syrup, tempting her thoughts to welcome in a juicy tidbit:

> Believe it is real
> Know it is true
> Feel how it will feel
> When it happens to you

"A sweet little diddy indeed," she smiled, welcoming a distant "indeed" to join her, and with that, she started walking again, newly adorned, feeling lifted and at ease. The landscape changed a little, and Stella continued to feel more and more disconnected from the world outside the geode.

It was an odd sensation to feel welcomed and comforted in this place, while also feeling estranged and somehow not where she belonged. The sensation of knowing this wasn't a place she was meant to stay long was encouraging; it helped her identify the things that were important to her well-being.

She needed to step onto soil again and back into the full spectrum of life. She was beginning to feel disoriented from herself in the limited colors and textures of this environment, so she started looking for an exit trail. Around the next bend was another choice: a continuation of the meandering path she was on or a slippery slope that seemed to lead elsewhere.

She asked herself earnestly which way to go and then tentatively placed a foot on the new path. There was no traction; she wouldn't be walking down this. Contemplating what was real in this upside-down moment, releasing fear and stepping into the feels, she said, "I am safe," out loud and heard a "yes" in reply. Stella straightened her crown, checked her pockets, made sure all was well, sat down and exclaimed, "Here I go!" which was echoed by a "Weeeeeee!" as she leaned into it and let go.

Spiraling Up

This slide was like a roller coaster! It wasn't particularly fast, but it went up and over and around, through the cascading curtains of vines, and loop-de-looped around the sparkling tree. Then it sent her into a steep pitch that swooped her over a broken edge and outside the geode. She was cast into the brightness of day as she gently slid down a hillside until the ground leveled out and she somersaulted onto the softest grass carpet she'd ever felt.

Stella sat there in the place she landed, unmoving. She was facing away from the other side of the tree she visited before entering the geode. She felt no pain, no worry, no fear, only curiosity about what she had just experienced. *Fun* wasn't the word—that was actually really hard. It was challenging and she was left feeling tired with a lot to process.

Stella spun around, still seated, but what was there was not any longer. The perspective had completely changed. The geode now looked like a typical hillside, covered in soil and grasses and wildflowers—no crystals, no blue light. What she had slid on now looked like a simple dirt path.

She saw the shape, felt the energy and, most importantly, *knew* it had happened. After all, she was still wearing the crown.

SYNERGY SWAMP
Remember Your Gifts and Use Them

The sun was in the afternoon sky, and Stella needed a bit of food and some time to be still after that experience. She eventually stood up and headed away from the hillside. Not far up, she saw a tree stump so enticing it was as if it had her name on it. Covered with moss and crooked like a hammock, it was calling her tired body towards it.

As she got closer, there was a small stream flowing underneath so she scooped up a handful of cold spring water and sipped. It was the most refreshing water she had ever tasted. It was like drinking the essence of the mountain; invigorating and eternal, with the subtle essence of cedar.

With each taste, she imagined hundreds of millions of trees from old-growth forests living and dying on the mountain, their healing oil seeping into the ground where it could gently permeate the waters. It was remarkable and delicious. *YUM*, she thought. She turned and sat in the woodland lounger with the stream at arm's length, her fingers dangling in it.

To the other side of her, she caught a glimpse of ruby red sparkling in the corner of her eye. To her surprise, it was a fresh berry—a plethora of them in fact! Ripe, fragrant and variegated tones of reds reflected the light of the sun on each shiny fresh globe. Without the

Spiraling Up

usual concern when eating wild berries, she popped one in her mouth and closed her eyes to enjoy the taste bud party.

The sweetness exploded first, followed by tart, savory and a bit of spice! All the flavors came through with just the right soft but not mushy texture. She was shocked at how satisfying it was too, despite its size. After only a few, she felt like she was eating enough to recharge and refill.

Of course, that would be after a little nap, she thought to herself. Quickly full and rehydrated, she closed her eyes and curled up into the cozy little haven. Clicks and murmurs entered her awareness. Did she hear talking? Was it a dream or was this happening around her? She did not wake regardless of the answer.

She did dream. Her resting mind wandered to friends and dear ones, warm feelings of those closest to her, memories of care and nurturing. She drifted to their support at her lowest moments. They gave her space yet were right there any time she needed them. The best of friends were not there just to do for her, but also help her do for herself. Some served the tasks of life, others served the spirit, and in thinking of all of them, her heart overflowed with the good stuff.

Her muscles softened. Each connection in her dream world that brought her light and love also brought her physical ease. The feelings were like a balm on sore muscles. It felt really nice.

As quickly as she fell asleep, she woke. Suddenly her eyes opened wide as if ready to take in the world. A smile stretched across her face. As she sat up, it became clear she had indeed been visited while sleeping.

Around her were several adorned items made from nature's offerings. There was no sign of who had left them, no footprints or notes, only the faint memory of activity that had found its way into her slumber.

She cupped a bit more water and nibbled a berry while she carefully and slowly examined the gifts. Each varied in size and was uniquely decorated. The first of three was a tall stick, something she could lean on for support. She noticed it had deep red bark, but unlike the Redwood, this was thin and soft as silk to the touch. *Walk steady with my staff,* she recalled from the night with her Ancient Grandmother. It offered insight into what was to come.

The stick had crooks and nooks, bends and bumps that perfectly aligned with her hand as she held it up in front of her. There were carvings on the bark, geometric symbols with strategically placed small colored stones embedded into the wood throughout. Given her journey so far, it seemed quite a practical, thoughtful and truly beautiful gift.

She shifted to the next, a small bark cube. Fitting into the palm of her hand, the rough exterior was made with flat pieces of dark, deeply ingrained bark. Each piece was notched to form a puzzle edge that neatly fit into the next to create a perfect container—a cleverly mischievous box that seemingly did not want to be opened! She had no desire to destroy it, so she shook it, smelled it and inspected it until finally setting it back down for delayed resolve. She then took a look at the last of the three: a sachet made of tree leaf and floral twine.

She untwisted the green vine twine, which had tiny fuzzy-ball flowers that acted like Velcro with each loop. *Quite a clever plant and use for it!* she thought. The leaf packet slowly expanded open, bursting with fragrances: Chamomile, Mint, Thyme, Eucalyptus and bright orange Calendula. She knew these plants and was connected to them; how peculiar that these should be the ones chosen! Each one was familiar for their healing and spiritual properties, each one something she might reach for in her real world if she needed the remedy they offered. Her curiosity piqued with this gift, and her enthusiasm and energy for what was next skyrocketed.

Spiraling Up

She stood from her lounging stump and gathered her new things to carry on up the path. With her new twine, she was able to lasso the puzzle box and sachet long and low across her body. Holding the stick as she imagined it was intended, she began to walk with it. It took only a few steps for Stella to realize how much better she felt. The rest, the nourishment and the surprises left her feeling light and at ease once again.

She was connecting this relaxed state to a feeling she'd been having more often. Was this her new normal? Was she staying above the horizon line Serophant had shown her? This state of being seemed to be her new being, in between the ups and downs, and she liked it. She felt recalibrated.

Never knowing what was next on this crazy adventure, she headed up the path with only a shimmering reflection of light catching her eye in the distance. Enjoying the scenery and casually strolling up the path, it felt like one of the quieter moments of her journey. There were no distractions, no curiosities, just the quiet hum of nature, the warm sun and unencumbered footsteps. She cruised along in the satisfaction of it all.

One step in front of the other with little change but the color of the path. From gravely grays to earthly browns, she noticed it was becoming greener. Not grassy, just green compact ground cover slowly expanding across the terrain in front of her. Moving deeper and deeper into emerald, she could feel the moisture on her skin. Her breath was heavy with humidity and a buzzing sound began to get louder…a buzz she immediately recognized.

Mosquitos! Oh, no—what was one were now 20, and her empty hand quickly became a swatter, flicking back and forth in defense of the constant attacks. She was so preoccupied, she failed to notice the ground cover begin to float beneath her feet.

SPLASH!

Mucky water spilled over her and continued to rise up to her ankle, locking her in place, so she jolted her knee up to lift her foot with all her might. This tugged her forward and off balance. She landed on her knees amidst some shallower muck.

Thankfully the momentum released her feet from the earthly vacuum. On the flip side: she was soaking wet and filthy again. Her hands were still clean, having held onto the staff she was able to stop herself. She took the moment to rearrange her treasures a bit higher. No longer hanging low at her hips, she tightened the vine so it hugged her chest. A little adjustment made all the difference. These small items in her care mattered, and with that breath, she felt a softening in her heart and a surge of golden pink light expand directly behind her new chest pack.

The sensation was warm and welcome. It also distracted her from the grime that covered her lower half. With another smile on her face, her mind flashed to a deep knowing that *from the muck grow the biggest blooms.*

In but a blink of an eye she found herself able to stand and move forward again with a lightness in her steps that did not exist a moment ago. *This is clearly healing mud,* she thought to herself, *surely better than the finest spas in all the lands!* This humored her as she slowly stepped forward with focused intention. She found relief from mosquitos at the parts of her covered in mud, but not wanting to cover her face and arms, she decided to use one of the gifts in her little satchel: Eucalyptus.

She carefully unbound the bundle and retrieved a few leaves from inside, trying not to drop anything when removing them. With everything in its place, she held the leaves to her nose, closed her eyes and inhaled their fragrance. When she opened her eyes, she was standing in a forested glen, dense with the tallest Eucalyptus trees she had ever

Spiraling Up

seen. Their towering narrow trunks ascended so high she could not see their tops, but she could hear them.

The leaves shook softly like maracas, shimmying and swaying with each other in an ancient song. She could not understand their words, but she felt their play, their rhythm and their telling of a very long story. The wind pushed against their narrow tips and gently bent the trunks too, creating synchronistic movement among them. *The song of the bending is the sound of life for a Eucalyptus, a symphony of strength, flexibility and connection.*

Each bend released a creaking and eeking sound as if the limbs had been still too long. Their stretching sounds reminded Stella of early morning, when closed eyelids start to let in light, skin is touched by the cool morning air and the body extends its reach to restart the senses and bring in a new day.

She was inspired by the grace of the Eucalyptuses and humbled by their gentle power. She felt like she was being welcomed home. The magnificence of the trees kept her attention looking up, until she noticed their fragrance enrobe her.

That brought her attention to a mist of sorts in the air, perhaps a fog, yet she was unsure if the moisture was from where she stood or what she saw; both seemingly very different places to occupy all at once. She was learning to allow these dual moments to overlap without barriers and be open to the revelations of insight, so she suspended her logic and allowed this multiverse to be.

The mist became an instrument to carry the Eucalyptus oils. She could see the dewiness float around and feel it gently land on her, leaving a sheen of protection. Her Grandmother taught her about the bug repellant gifts of this lanky tree and now she received their magic directly. Each dewdrop connecting into the other on her skin soothed and sealed her in a clear coat, safe from the siege of the winged stinging swamp things. There was also an olfactory spell; the oils protected her lungs from the damp and lifted her spirits to the treetops. She was armored.

In a blink she was standing in the mud again. Now, she also felt revived and repellent; at least to the mosquitos. Her mind felt sharp, and she moved faster, no longer trudging along through the swamp.

The source of the water was a wall on her right, seeping through a steep sheer edge. It was a narrow valley path where land and water met, and their synergy created a unique environment. It appeared the water had saturated the soil and gravel path in a way that actually protected the rocks from erosion, and the biomes it created carried down the cliff walls and fed the fields and forests she had passed through on her journey thus far.

To her left, a narrow strip of dense wild grass and brush occasionally cleared enough for her to see it was clinging to the top of the next steep drop down. She believed where she stood eventually became the crystal-clear falls she bathed in so luxuriously. It may even be where it begins. The idea that this verdantly opaque synergizing swamp helped create it didn't go unnoticed. "Let the good stuff flow," she said to no one.

One experience feeds the next—that she understood. After Falling-Up Hill, she was well aware that what she had learned, what she did with that awareness and how she evolved from it was up to her. She created her world, and her world created her. She laughed at her circular logic. "If not for me, I am nothing." She let the rest go to simply enjoy the mosquito-free mud path.

Ahead was a brilliant light source that was pointing outwardly in every direction. She felt like she was walking towards a star seeing the piercing white light fractured in a million beams. She looked forward to what could possibly be so big and bright up the path.

Spiraling Up

She pulled her focus to her next footsteps, back to the present, feeling temporarily blinded by the light ahead. Her grumbling hunger took her attention next as her body made clear it was time to eat. When she lifted her gaze, to her joy, she saw new colors appear around her. Little dots of blue and pink berries robustly popped out from the brush as if to say, "Pick me!"

She collected a large handful of wild snacks and found a boulder worn smooth enough to sit on. Resting comfortably, she reached into her satchel and pulled out the fresh mint. Breathing it in as if it were oxygen, she tore bits of the leaves and folded each berry into one like a tiny colorful taco.

The powershot of flavor woke up her senses! She shook her head and yelled "WOO!" with a laugh. The mint tasted like the color green; refreshing and vital. The berries made Stella's face squish uncontrollably as she giggled through the tartness. She felt nourished, eased, replenished and giddy. She was swaddled with a sense of well-being and positivity, knowing that her needs would be met even if she didn't know how. She felt cared for.

With that new appreciation, she stood back up and carried forward towards an end of this passage that she could not see but knew very well was coming. She walked easier with her staff, thankful for all it offered on this trek. It seemed like a full day had passed, though she could not be sure; she was only sure she was still wet and ready to step out of the mud.

The landscape began to change. Thicker thickets replaced the rock wall as it thinned down to a few boulders and revealed a radiant field of flowers around its hidden bend. Still in the mud, every step became firmer beneath her feet. *At last*, she thought, *it is over*.

The vibrant field was a shocking contrast to the swamp; she hadn't realized it was so dim there. Blinking quickly to recalibrate, she stum-

Synergy Swamp

bled around boulders, towards a new sound of flowing water. It grew steadily louder than the trickle on the cliff's edge, so she followed it, hoping she could wash off this day. She ambled along until she found a nook that would be her place for the evening.

She was next to a field of brilliantly orange Calendula, the same as in her bundle; it was growing, and glowing all around her. When she reached her chosen spot, she pushed the staff into the soil to stand on its own for a while.

The crusted layers of her clothes were drying and they had become painfully rigid to move in. Emptying her pockets with a new sense of urgency, she placed each item side by side on a rock shelf perfectly suited for such a thing.

A flush of shame that she had already forgotten what she was carrying came over her. How could she forget? *What she carried held no weight, no burden, no distractions,* yet every time she reached into her small side pocket she returned with something else. Was that the point? *If I recall what I need when I need it, do I really need to keep inventory?* She let the shame go as quickly as it came.

When she held the Double R Starbit, she felt Dirt and MacA AyA's generous spirits. Her mind began to dance with Serophant as she grabbed his gift and recalled his message *Play is Joy is Love is Qubes.* There was LaLu Narock from Lady JuJu, and the small vessel of cleansing waters—a token from Kuan Yin and Madam AuraCull.

She took a closer look at the satchel she carried too. The stitching shimmered like spider webs in the rain, and she was overcome with the belief that it was Faerie thread, so she decided it was. And she still didn't know what was in the box. Such a peculiar collection of little things with big intentions.

She dared not delay much longer as she didn't want to lose the light or get stuck in her clothes, so she peeled of the hardened fabric and left the pile for later. Still wearing the key to Serophant's garden, she opted to leave it on, grabbed the cleansing vessel and headed towards the sound of running water. The dirt path narrowed and lined with flowers so tall, they nearly kissed her cheeks as she passed.

To her delight, it was a hot spring. She took a deep body-filling breath and stretched her foot towards the water while standing on the edge. One toe, then five. The water temperature was perfect. Stepping down cautiously, she felt her body become one with the soothing liquid warmth. She settled on a rock shelf seat neck deep and rested her head on a mossy pad at the edge. She felt rewarded.

The golden Calendula also hugged the pool's edge, along with Chamomile and Thyme—the same plants she had been given. Each one seemed to bend over and reach for the water but not quite touch it. Instead, the steam rose and clung to them, warming the soft petals and releasing their natural remedies. Their essence filled Stella with calm; each inhale left her senses soothed and her body tranquil.

Calendula nurtured and strengthened the resilience of her body; Chamomile soothed and calmed her mind and Thyme sprung her thoughts towards loving connections and wisdom. All that she could think was *YUM*.

Stella had set the cleansing vessel down next to her when she stepped in, but she found it floating in the pool, like a cork on the water, and left it bobbing on the surface from the constant motion created by the freshwater spring. There was also a gurgling from below and as Stella investigated, she realized the heat was coming from deep within the mountain. *The gentlest warmth comes from deep within.*

The waters surrendering over the rocks at the surface, on the other hand, were cold like ice, streaming from the mountain peak under flora and fauna to this perpetual spa. Her deep breathing continued as the magic of awareness unfolded. Each moment of new clarity sparked another and another.

The dance of water led her attention to the songs of birds. They were abundant and in harmony, carried on the winds through the leaves which added to the melodies. The Conductor had introduced her to full spectrum vision and the harmonic messages of nature. So, Stella listened and bore witness to her surroundings, open to the messages that might seep into her quieting mind. It was then the floating vessel opened.

The liquid Pearls of Illumination slithered around Stella and began to float up and over her skin as if she was the water. It wasn't long before her entire body was covered. As it offered no sensation or concern so she simply relaxed into it and shimmered while she soaked.

Across from where she had entered the pool was a smooth carved out spot under an awning of rock and shrub and atop a patch of densely thick moss. When she stood, the pearl essence clung to her like a body suit shimmering in the waning light.

When she stepped out of the water, the shimmer evaporated with the steam, leaving her feeling released from the little things on the surface. In that moment she was reminded how Madam AuraCull had told her it would help her walk lightly.

She moved to the mossy mat, as soft as any bed, sat down and felt the heat again. The same source energy warming the pool also warmed the soil. A slip of earth allowed her to walk back to her belongings which she collected before returning to her camp for the night. The clothes were not fit to wear, so she tossed them into the waters for a soak of their own.

After a bit, she thought it best to get her laundry done. Harkening back to the days of washboards, she knocked her clothes against the rocks, loosened the hard day and worked some clean into them.

Taking a chance they would dry overnight, she laid them on a heated patch of soil and sat back down, alone and naked.

Lying bare on the warmed earth, she reached for the edge of the moss and pulled a long piece of it over her as she rolled to her side. She flashed images in her mind of all sorts of stories featuring naked women in the woods. She did not feel like dancing or running. She wasn't timid or cold, hunting or hunted. She felt natural, safe and like it was the best option in the moment, so she decided it was okay.

The evening light washed over the field mixing its golds with warm pinks, as if mirroring the colors that filled her heart, connecting her to deep love. Curling up cozy and restored, giving herself full permission to relax, she quickly fell asleep as the sun passed beyond the mountain's edge.

CANYON OF MIRRORS
The Depth of Reflection is Equal to the Matter

As she woke, she realized she was still wearing the crown. A great sleep restored Stella's energy and faith in her ability to complete this journey. She unfurled from the mossy cover and hopped into the pool for a morning dip. Her clothes had dried overnight and were quite perfectly resting next to some of those delicious wild berries she had snacked on before.

Fulfilling as honor, light as ease, sweet as joy and tart as growth, her thoughts popped like each berry in her mouth. She was present and grateful, greeting the light of the morning sun. What was golden at day's end was now the color of lemons; bright and cheery.

The difficulties of the swamp had melted away with the awareness of the gifts she effortlessly carried. The only effort was in remembering they were there for her and the self-berating that came with forgetting. She could stop her self-chastising and instead focus on integrating a deeper truth: *Each gift has a purpose, and the awareness presents itself right on time.* "IF!" she hollered out with a knowing smile, "I am open to receive it."

While lounging in her hot bath, she acknowledged that when she flipped her thoughts from shame for forgetfulness of her own resources to forgiving herself and allowing grace, she was able to move forward with ease. "I am learning," she said, proud of her new perspective.

Each thought passing through confidence strengthened her intuitive muscles, allowing her to express the possibilities of a chosen life from a place that can create it.

The next step was to get out of the bath and get ready for the day's journey. She was up, out and dressed in no time, but something had changed. When she lifted her pants, there was a small patch of seedlings popping up for their first bit of sunlight. It was then she realized the seedy mud ball had been left in a pocket! Stella had unknowingly planted a new garden and she wished into the universe that Lady JuJu would find her way there to enjoy it.

She then collected all the gifts and reached for the staff. The staff, however, did not budge, so she stopped to evaluate it. The base, which was covered in mud, had solidified as hard as concrete. Like a fence post, the staff would not move. Then she noticed something else—there was a new leaf near the top of it, above the carvings and stones; it was a sign of rebirth.

As she stared, light peeked through the canopy onto the embedded stones, making them sparkle. The sight brought tears to her eyes; it felt precious. She said a blessing for new gardens and sturdy trees to feel complete in the moment and then turned to carry on.

There were a lot of aha moments drumming through her head, and the open path offered space to process them. Once she passed the field, the glimmer of a thousand light bursts came into view again. It was mesmerizing, alluring, enchanting and just up ahead.

Her stride became a glide. It was so easy and fluid. Each step was no longer something she felt her body take. She eased into each one with a lean as if she were skating. The ground seemed smoother too; as one foot slid out, the other followed suit. Enjoying this new pace and movement, she hadn't noticed she was walking on the sky.

Soon there was no top, no bottom, no end or beginning; she was floating above it all! What she thought was trees was actually towering mirror walls. The starburst of light she had been seeing was the sun's reflected rays. She had arrived at a canyon of mirrors.

This environment carried only a simulation of what was warm and comforting; in reality, this was a cold place whose purpose was to be a stark illusion. Some areas were pristine and perfectly glimmered back what they saw, while other parts were dense and the images they reflected were muted. Some walls were imposing shards, some were opaque like sea glass, others were crystal clear. The areas also varied in texture. Smooth surfaces met jagged ridges, and broken corners distorted reflections into a kaleidoscope of images bouncing back and forth, smaller and smaller into themselves.

The effect was hypnotizing; staring at it pulled her into an infinite smallness. As she had done throughout the journey, Stella embraced the experience and trusted her fate was destined to be good. She pulled her focus back and continued to walk steadily with her eyes watching a few steps ahead.

As she moved into the canyon, it shifted to a deeply saturated reflection of sunset. Could she have been there that long already? Gentle colors reflected on themselves, layering into rich jewel tones, adding a warmth to the space that was missing. In that light, a shift in the reflections also took form. What had been a reflection of the present soon became a timeless window of self-images. Much like those of a carnival fun house, these reflections weren't flattering to her. It irked her that in such beauty, she was forced to see her distorted self and all her cracks.

On Falling-Up Hill, she had fine-tuned her awareness of what her body was telling her before her mind could process and spell it out. In this moment, she knew what she was seeing was not just a play of the glass. Consciously expediting her pace, she wanted to move through this quickly.

She wasn't interested in a deep dive here. She did not want anything to do with these portrayals. She knew exactly what they were; projections of what others told her she was and images of what she allowed others to define her as. She immediately felt a resonant NO throughout her body. *No, no, no.*

She knew these images represented other people's versions that she had laid over herself like shrink wrap. These personas did not align with her own version of herself now, nor did they then either, but now she could say NO. "AHA!" she said, followed by, "Phew! These reflections show me how I allowed myself to create my world with their limitations and boundaries. I minimized myself in order to achieve the expectations of someone else's *shoulds*." She felt obstinate.

Stella was not these images; the clarity not only emanated from her third eye—it was her stomach, her heart and her tingling spine that all said NO. Most of the streaming on the glass screens were the versions Momma said she should have been, had to be; things other than who Stella truly was. She also saw versions of herself that her late husband labeled her with; unkind names from the mouth of a troubled man, meant to leave her feeling as diminished and defeated as he felt himself. Deep down, Stella knew herself better than that and she believed in herself enough to know they weren't right, and still she spent years ineffectively battling the dysfunction of these important relationships.

The images kept coming, like the entrepreneur who didn't quite make it. Then there were all the other versions: too fat, too mouthy, too smart, too loud and too much. Each one was splashed upon the towering spears. Standing there, she rejected every single one of them.

"I know who you are," she spoke with resolve to them all, "I know where you come from, and I know where you reside in me. You are a reflection of other people's needs and judgments." Waving her hands expressively, basically telling them off, she declared, "You. Are. Not. Me." Stella stood tall, regained her composure and began a walk out of the canyon. "I am not having it. I release it all—it never belonged to me anyway."

Not willing to look back, she continued past the remaining displays until she noticed the ground changing once again. No longer needing to focus on her footsteps, she looked up just before the path hit a wall. She stopped and found herself face-to-face with an eight-foot mirror.

Stella took a deep breath and stepped back, allowing herself to see herself fully. What she saw back was her, truly her, and it made her cry. She wasn't crying over the dusty and mismatched baggy clothes or the bits of moss and sticks coming out of her hair. She was crying because she was overcome with the sight of her own authenticity, the real deal, her soul self.

She was overflowing with a sense of well-being, as the tears came from what she saw in her own eyes. The reflection of self ricocheted layer upon layer amongst flecks of gold in her hazel eyes. She felt the warmth of her own love, as if she finally accepted herself as she was. "Hello," she said sincerely.

As quickly as the moment happened, it was gone. Left with her hand reaching towards the mirror and the glow of her high heart upon her rosy cheeks, she felt settled with a profound sense of self and the one opinion she could now filter everything through: hers. "I did that," she said, looking at herself with accomplishment. "From this day forward, forevermore, may I know myself this clearly." She set the intention for herself, adding a *Reality Reset* for good measure.

Stable and sure, she peered around the towering wall and followed the path out.

Stella felt proud of herself. She found the path quickly through the Canyon of Mirrors with a sense of calm and discernment. She knew what was right for her and made those choices with confidence in the moment. Keeping her focus, she didn't let the environment affect her further. When she was shown who she wasn't, it was also a spotlight on who she was; the contrast came fast and clear. She felt seen.

THE EDGE OF SHADOWS AT TIPPING POINT

A Night at the Inn

The sun was indeed setting when she finally reached the end of the canyon. She carried up the path, hoping a place to rest would present itself; a comfortable tree, a patch of moss or perhaps a little cave by the river. Where she stood, the ground was razed and vacant of life; like her, the soil seemed exhausted.

Stella was empowered by her choices and clarity with the images in the mirrors, but it was still a tiring process. The surfaces she was now encountering required extra care to traverse, the focus was intense and her body felt stiff and depleted from it all. As she shuffled along, plopping one foot in front of the other, she noticed her surroundings change. Overhead was darkness; she assumed she had walked under a canopy of trees, but she could not say for sure. There was no movement, no sounds and no light between leaves. As she wandered up the way, she saw a single flicker ahead, a beacon in the gloaming.

She continued towards the light. It seemed further and further though she thought she was getting closer, something that seemed to keep happening in response to her eagerness to move ahead. At last, the light began to get bigger into view. What looked to be a sliver of a moon shimmering in a starless sky had the words "Edge of Shadows Inn" underneath it.

"Stay for a night, remember for a lifetime," the placard on the door said, a little ominously. She pulled on the heavy wooden door using a twisty knotted handle made from a branch. She strained against the weight of massive hinges that creaked as the door opened. When she stepped in, she was knocked back by a surprising and intense aroma…cookies!

The long journey all at once caught up with her as the whiff of caramelized sugar instantly stripped away her layers and left her bare, at least figuratively. She continued in and heard a scuffle, then a muffled, "You're here! Wonderful. Right on time." A pink-cheeked, cheerful expeditor of comfort promptly set a steaming plate of fresh-baked goodness in front of her on the counter.

"I am the InnerKeep, and I am so glad to greet you, Stella!" "You were expecting me?" she replied. "At the Edge of Darkness, we don't see a star very often. I saw your sparkle heading my way for quite some time. I hope you like cookies." Of course she did. Stella smiled gratefully and enjoyed the delicious treat with a well-deserved "Yum."

"Ahhh. That is the sound of the heart! Thank you," the InnerKeep smiled back, "I can see you're tired, but I do need to prepare you for your journey this evening." "Journey?" Stella said with a full mouth, "I am done with this day! The only journey left is the one to a place where I can lay my head down to sleep. I hope I have found that place," Stella said, confused, through cookie crumbs and exhaustion.

"I have a room ready for you and despite your *reservations*," said with a wink of innkeeper humor, "a new journey is about to begin. This is the Edge of Shadows Inn at Tipping Point and those who wander here are called to shadows within themselves." Stella let out a massive sigh, indicative of one who believed they at last had checked off the boxes of their day only to find another list of things yet undone.

"No rest for the wicked?" Stella jested. "Indeed," the InnerKeep said in quick retort, "The wicked rest easily here. It is those who wish to live in light who will face their demons while they slumber." "Demons!? Wait a minute, what do you mean *demons*?" Stella gasped, "I just want to sleep!" The sounds of apprehension and frustration rounded out her exclamation.

With that, the InnerKeep turned and shuffled back through the doorway, returning a moment later with a teapot and two chipped cups. Nodding with a glance towards the nook nearby, Stella followed, carrying the cookie plate with her. When they each sat, the tea was served and the insight continued without further delay.

"Do not fear, Stella. Trust the path you are on is for the highest good. Some demons may battle for your attention in dark places. Mischievous and deceiving, they can be the distractions of others you may still be attached to, attempting to guide you away from your focus. Look at them as a way to strengthen yourself against those who try to redirect you. Give them no more than required of you and follow your light to come back.

"If they are your demons, you will feel their presence much stronger. If your path is one that haunts you, then it may feel like the battle of a lifetime. Facing demons can be terrifying, yet they have a weakness. They can only find you in the shadows. If they feel too strong to face, you can leave them behind until you are ready. Sometimes you need armor or an army to fight them. If you cannot go it alone, do not. Some demons might still be left in the deepest parts of you because the battle is too risky, and that's okay. Even if they never leave, it is up to you to choose the light, moment by moment, day by day. And once you do, you can step beyond the darkness and beyond their reach."

Spiraling Up

After each tossed another cookie in their mouth, the guidance continued, "*Daemons*, on the other hand, are spirits who walk a middle path to guide and serve you, to help you find the place where you balance your capacity to serve yourself and others as you choose, and to show you how your choices affect your path."

"Daemons share the emotions of the human experience. Everyone has a compass inside them that points them somewhere, though many use someone else's and never truly follow their own. Tonight, you will calibrate your compass."

Stella interjected, "I don't dabble in darkness or mess with demons, and I have never heard of a *day-mun*."

"It is time, dear Stella." Grabbing a last cookie and leaving the rest behind, they stood. Stella followed the InnerKeep's lead as they headed towards a door. "Right and wrong are subjective to the outside world. This journey is about your inside world—what is and what is not aligned with your truth—and only you can determine that.

"Some people are born to do horrific things, and even they are part of the balance of the world. I assure you, my dear, you are not born for that, but you do have a purpose. You are a star of light and love, dear Stella, and I believe tonight you will discover what that means for you."

I always want to choose light, Stella thought. Then the InnerKeep's voice interrupted her inner dialogue. "Welcome to the Edge of Shadows Inn, Stella. You are in the right place at the right time. Your room awaits you." And with that, The InnerKeep welcomed her onto the top landing of a wooden staircase, and they began to descend.

Winding down a series of steps through a zig-zagging breezeway, Stella learned she was stepping her way down the edge of a cliff. Sometimes there were openings through which she briefly gazed outward at the stars. After one zag, or zig, she saw the tip of a boulder, fine as a needle, that widened into a smooth basin of stone beneath it.

They paused on the next landing that seemed to be outside of every door they passed. This one overlooked the sculpture that Stella just noticed and the InnerKeep began to explain what it was. "Over time, beads of water dripped upon the stone basin, bit by bit, descending from the mountain that birthed it. It flowed along the cracks and weaknesses and created new ones until it wore through, and the water found a release, severing what was once whole."

The words fell upon Stella with the weight of being severed and broken in her own life. Was it her desire to feel whole again that had brought her to the Inn? The InnerKeep continued, "And ever since it broke, the basin and the tip have found their own way, each with a purpose that serves them, each other and the greater good. We like to call that a win-win-win around these parts."

Stella felt an understanding that when a barrier breaks and the energy flows, it can allow the freedom for what was meant to be and the possibility of a new connection to what once was but is no more.

Further and further down, they stepped, and Stella could not wrap her head around it! *How many stories is this place? What kind of room is on the edge of a cliff?* Feelings of fear and anxiety were creeping in; she knew them immediately. As for now, she was keeping this to herself.

The InnerKeep continued, seemingly unaware of Stella's emotional shift, until she glanced back and reminded Stella, "Do not fear. You are safe—even at the Tipping Point." Stella clung to those words like the railing she held, and they continued down, down, down.

When at last the InnerKeep stopped, Stella was relieved to see she wasn't at the bottom; other rooms laid deeper yet, and for some reason, that gave her comfort.

Spiraling Up

They stopped at a door with no number. There was only a single silver star in the center. "Remember it is *those with the most to gain that face the greatest challenges*. Unlock your shackles and set yourself free. Dream well, Starlight."

Upon those words being spoken, the door was opened and as soon as Stella stepped in, the door closed behind her. Her imagination had been running wild with the ominous warnings leading there, so she was pleased to find a warm and comforting room awaited her. As if they knew she was coming, the room wafted with her favorite scents. It had cozy, soft linens and lighting. It all soothed her quickly.

She perused the quaint space. The wooden furniture bound with twine was rustic and solid. The mattress appeared to be densely fluffy, soft and supportive; inviting her to climb in. Her eyes moved across the irregular shaped room with stone and wood walls.

There was a single frame showcasing a large embroidered canvas over the bed. It displayed a pair of silver thread shackles next to a rusty-looking key with a red rose wrapped around it, with real thorns woven in with the utmost care. Hand-stitched on a piece of dense fabric, it read, "New shackles hold old pain. Hidden keys unlock them."

Stitched in more silver thread at the bottom, it read, "trust thyself, heal thyself, free thyself." *Is this the next key I'm supposed to find?*

She was impressed by the artistry. "That's a lot to stitch," she said aloud. Not putting much thought into keys or the last words the InnerKeep said, the "coincidence" of shackles had been lost in the moment, and she mindlessly undressed and crawled into bed.

Quickly settled, she reached up towards the lamp and spun the knob. With a simple *click*, she was in darkness. "Why did I do that?" she said audibly, immediately regretting her decision to not leave the gentle light on. Instantly uncomfortable, she promptly turned the light back on and wrapped herself in the blanket, seeking relief from this vulnerability taking over her. It helped, but only a little.

At first, she didn't know what happened. She was startled by an emptiness and lack in the room. In that split second of darkness, something changed, there was now a hollow chill. She attempted to close her eyes repeatedly, but each time she did images of terror, worse than the darkness, flooded her:

World chaos

Domestic violence

Cruelty

Suffering

She felt the pain that came with each one, and her muscles cramped. She contorted her body, seeking comfort, but she could not find it. Flashes of pain crackled behind visions of sorrow, like the worst movie ever made was streaming in front of her and she did not have the controls. She felt more and more frightened and alone until it all suddenly stopped.

Stella was no longer in the same room. Now she sat in a vacant space with an absence of light; a void, a holding place. She was now shackled, seated with her legs bound together at her ankles. She could stand and her arms were free, but she remained motionless; feeling vulnerable and alone.

The idea of being alone was desirable once the darkness became occupied. She sensed a figure loomed near, barely visible as a vague silhouette between shades of night. She dared not look at the entity or engage. Withholding all of her energy, she tried to deprive it from consuming her power. It was then that her body forcibly spasmed

Spiraling Up

into the fetal position and she fell off the chair, only to find there was no floor.

She felt fear weigh heavy on her chest, gulping for air as if it was unattainable. Dragged further and further from what she longed for—connection, love, trust. These lifelines were now beyond her reach and the sinking feeling consumed her.

Sinking

An unknown something that thrived in her hidden places had welcomed her as she inadvertently entered a portal there. She had hit a new bottom. When she cried out for help and declared that she was alone and vulnerable, her call was answered like the rescue of a crying lamb by a wolf, with a chilling "You are not alone." "NO!" Stella screamed out. She was filled with regret for being here but her refusal to give in was stronger. Her body was convulsing; it wasn't just saying NO, it was SCREAMING it! She squirmed and clenched. Then her eyes felt forced open as she was furled into a ball. Curled tight on her side, Stella's head shook like a bobble as she yelled out, "NO, NO, NO!" The figure quietly motioned for her to rise and come to it.

"This is NOT what I want," she yelled at the being, her heart beating the rhythm of ancient war drums. She caught her breath again. "I do not call upon darkness in need. I will not let you in." At the top of her lungs, she yelled out, "My feelings and words are not an invitation to you! EVER!" With tears running down her cheeks, she quieted her voice, "Never. I am light. You are dark." Only then did she realize she had descended to this dark place by her own actions. It did not come for her; she had come to it.

Her breathing felt feral, but her body released the pain with that awareness. She was regaining control of herself. She slowly unfurled and began sitting up to compose herself. She refused the dark side, yet this anger and fear were the openings. *Darkness is not a place, it's a state of mind.* It was not the entity that must leave this space; it was her. *Follow my light to go back—isn't that what the InnerKeep said?* She stretched her arms, preparing to stand and find another way, when she realized her hand was not empty.

In this holding space of nothingness, she now held LaLu Narock. As she gazed upon it, she heard a humming sound she didn't realize

Spiraling Up

she was making. A deep sound vibrated from her chest, activating her heart and beyond. She could see LaLu Narock change; it reacted to her resonance and expanded into a blinding brilliant beam to cut through the bleak like a sword. As her hum grew more intentional the light within the stone expanded.

Suddenly she was alone again.

A Dark Portal

Still sitting, Stella sensed a softness growing in the space. No longer steeped in black, it became a mottled gray and now felt neutral. The stone still gently pulsed a white light, and her body went limp. She lay onto her back with a deep breath and full body gratitude for finding her way out of that place…and for her solitude. The pulsing light filled the space, like water fills a fish tank, and as the light elevated, so did she. When at last she stood, her shackles fell off.

The Edge of Shadows at Tipping Point

The light was on in the room when she opened her eyes. The experience she had was visceral. Still in bed, her body was sure it happened, yet her mind could hardly believe. Did she really descend to such a place? Was it all a vivid dream? She decided she didn't need to know. It was a very profound and disturbing night, and that was where she chose to leave it.

Her demons had been warned. There was NO state of mind she would EVER be in that was an invitation for them to join her. Every part of her spirit held that truth. She now understood she had the capacity for such travel, but she hoped that would be the end of that as she never intended to do it again.

Still feeling sleep call her in, she recalled how her footsteps on the staircase felt heavy. The conversation over tea and cookies had a tone that Stella was beginning to realize created anxiety and fear in her long before she put her head on that pillow, which she suspected was the intention.

Did I create that experience simply by allowing the ickyness of my shadows to take over? "Yes, I did," she affirmed, "I did that. I created a space to face my darkness, and in that space, I found the light to lead me back. I felt weak, like someone who had given up and no longer believed in their own power, and that was how I got there."

As she trailed into thought, she was seeing how her fears, triggers and traumas could ignite despair, an invitation to the dark and one of few bridges that could be used to reach her. The choice was up to her. When doubt crept in, she could speak to herself with insight and clarity. She had just discovered she could travel through both wonderful and scary places but with light in her heart to guide her, she would not get lost. She had been there and done that.

There is no light without darkness. Shadows balance the scale, though it need not be feared for merely being a dark place. Like all else, she could honor it for what it was and do with it what served the greater good. "The win-win-win!" she exclaimed, calling back insight from the InnerKeep. She had her bearings again. She was ready for some rest and did not have any hesitations about turning off the lamp.

The glow of sunrise eventually brightened the room once more, and Stella woke feeling like an army of one, triumphant in the battle for her soul. The portal she unintentionally opened had been closed—sealed, even. Certain this was not the last battle she would have in life, Stella now understood that how she responded to negative energy would determine her outcomes, as much as the battle itself. She could protect herself without destroying herself in the process. She felt victorious.

With each breath and reflection guiding her back to awareness of her strengths and gifts, she felt capable, rested and content. Pulling back the blankets, feeling the cool morning air on her skin, she took a deep breath and welcomed the new day.

Once dressed, her mind went to the coin in her pocket, which she grabbed without further thought, closed her eyes and said, "All portals to darkness in this lifetime or any others are closed. So be it. RICH." After a pause, she continued, "As if by magic, light will shine upon my shadows to expand my awareness for the best and highest outcomes. So be it. RACE." Then, she finished with a robust "Reality Reset."

She was a little surprised by the attuned request that spilled out of her so easily, and she gave herself a little pat on the back for simply remembering to do that. She gathered her belongings and was ready to check out from this strange lodging. Reaching for the door to leave, she paused in front of a small mirror. Yes, she still had on the crown, and it made her laugh out loud. Looking herself in the eyes, she said:

The Edge of Shadows at Tipping Point

I am strong, even when scared
I am safe, even when alone
I am heard, even when silent
I am my own destiny maker
AND
I will carry on with my badass self

THE ANSWER KEY

Integrate What You Have Always Known and Finally Understand

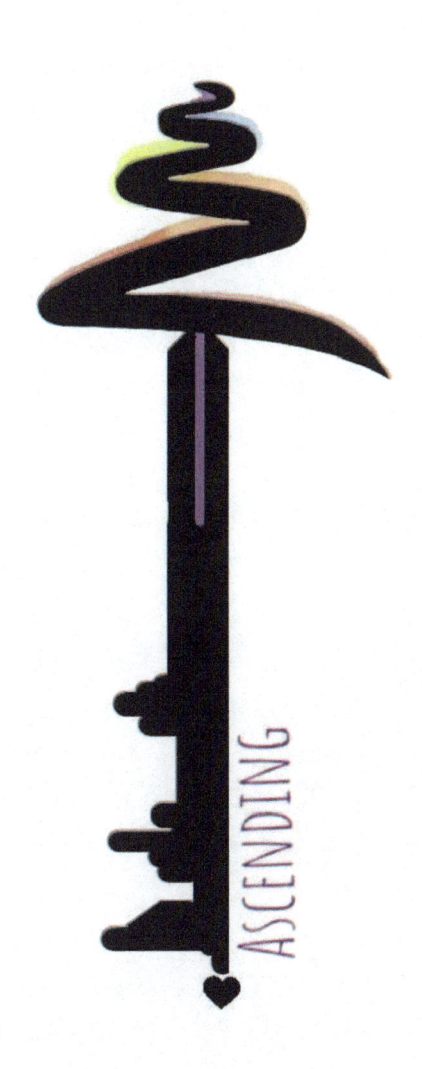

ASCENDING

A NEW DAY

The Goddess and the Dragon

Stella opened the door from her room and stepped out to head up the staircase towards the lodge. As she turned towards the day, her eyes fell upon her next place to be. The magnet in her compass locked onto it, without thought or intention. It was a single red chair in a circle within a field of tall grass. Next to it, a plume of smoke slowly swirled up. A sense of urgency overtook her and all she could think of was how she must sit there before someone else did.

It was quite a distance to the ground from where she stood on the cliffside and she wasn't sure how she'd get there, but she knew she had to. She had no idea why this feeling overtook her for that chair; it was unlike any she'd ever felt before. As she settled her mind on this sudden change of direction, she focused on where she was.

Where the stairs heading down continued, there was only a shadow. It was simply uninviting, and she knew she was not going that way. As she looked towards the staircase she came down, it was gone. No steps, no landings, no other doors. Instead, she was staring at a massive trunk and seemed to be standing on a wide and stable branch, as if she were an angel on the shoulder of the tree.

When she looked down towards the chair again, a wooden footbridge was revealed. It was made of vines and branches, bound and knotted. It even had railings to hold as it gently arched down towards

Spiraling Up

the field of grass not far from the chair. She was now being called in a new direction and was ready to be on her way; excited for her next destination despite having no idea why.

These realizations popped like corn in her mind. Little kernels of clarity ready for her to consume them. *Pop, pop, pop.* She noticed a tingly mist that smelled of tule fog, capturing the essence of fresh soil and damp moss on cold stone. She could almost taste nature's elements. There was silence in the air that accompanied the pale, sleepy sky; it shushed her as if to say her world had not yet awoken.

There were no more thoughts of last night and no new thoughts of breakfast. She had but one thing on her mind: *Sit in that chair!* She simply knew that once she did, the rest would sort itself out. *Get. To. That. Chair.* She confidently traversed the root bridge with laser focus on the destination. This was not merely a morning jaunt or a fun idea, she was being pulled with intention. She was being summoned.

This was a very strange feeling indeed. It was like a gravitational pull, a momentum beyond her own accord. At the edge of the field the grass stood ankle high and transitioned to taller and taller blades. The tips tickled her arms as she held them high to keep the grass off of her face. She could see the sky begin to wake around her when the grass turned into a field of greens as the shades of evening were at last cast off.

The smell of smoke came on the shifting breeze as she approached the small clearing where the chair eagerly awaited her arrival. Her eyes were focused on it as she turned and stumbled right over someone sleeping, "Oh! I am so sorry! I didn't see you there! Are you okay?" The words tumbled out of her much like she nearly tumbled over him.

The sleepy humble man, wrapped in what looked like a tribal blanket, could only be seen by a flashing shimmer which became a peeking eye underneath a woolen cap. Beneath the layers, a voice graciously welcomed her to sit anywhere she'd like by the fire. She beelined to the red chair that she believed woke her from her slumber and called her there.

Her host slowly rustled himself up, happy to greet the morning sun alongside her. The fire felt warm and comforting, and once seated, Stella was immediately content, no longer having any need to do anything else. She was driven to be there, and upon arrival, her motor stopped.

Despite the intensity of her dramatic, dark night, she woke into anew. She did not wake the same person who laid her head down the night before. She was altered. There was a sense of relief that a much deeper transformation was taking place. She also knew she did not need to find all the answers in the moment.

Her new acquaintance was now sitting nearby, feeding the fire its breakfast of branches. Stella once again apologized for the startling wake-up. "I am the Guardian of the Flame," he said proudly, "I tend it through the night, to keep it safe and welcoming to any who are called to it." "Called?" *A funny choice of words,* she thought. "What do you mean?" she asked.

She listened as he told the tales of his evening just a few hours earlier, around the same time she felt like she fought for her soul in a tiny room not far away. "There was a gathering overnight, as happens most nights, though last night was anything but typical," he started, "Last night we had a coven of witches, heading to a congress of magical folks somewhere over the edge of view." He pointed beyond the cresting sun. "You see, I am one of many guardians, and we never know which fire we will tend to or for how long or who we'll meet or what we'll learn." He paused for a breath, then continued, "But I do know I was meant to be here now."

Spiraling Up

Stella caught a glimpse of his smile as he said those words, and again, she saw a shimmer, this time across his cheek, perhaps the reflection of the sunrise. With a smile eager to hear more, she nodded as he continued. "In the evening the fire is hot, stoked for cooking and warmth, and on nights like last, a bit of spirits come about," he said with a wink and a rise of a cup that looked to be handmade of mud and fire, "We had a grand party before they carried on down the way."

He seemed to have reminded himself to offer her a cup of what he was having, which was a fermented berry mash with spring water. Happily accepting the tangy concoction, she was captivated in the moment and enjoying all it offered. He continued, "By the firelight, they sang to the stars, asking for their light to guide them on their journeys through the night. They danced with merriment and summoned the Goddess Stella while having a great time."

As he spoke, he looked up to see her eyes widen with awe then continued to speak of the carefree exchange of kindnesses when the travelers shared their meal with him. "Where are my manners?" he said. Reaching his hand out, he introduced himself, "There are no strangers at my fire. I am Daimon Glenn. Forest Dragon, Keeper of Fire, Protector of Trees, welcome morning traveler." Reaching back, she said, "I am Stella," smiling as she got to witness his eyes widen with awe.

The handshake slowed down as they stared at each other until finally letting go and leaning back into their chairs. She then told him her story of the InnerKeep, the demon and how she woke, summoned to be where she sat now. They both humbly agreed it was all VERY cool.

"I am no goddess, but it's still quite amazing I felt called here," Stella felt the need to clarify. "Of course you are," he corrected, "and the fact you were called here is your validation. Own your Feminine

Divine and claim your Goddess Power, Stella. Do not be blind to who you are." Shocked at his response, she thought it was arrogant to call herself a goddess, but that wasn't it at all.

"The Feminine Divine? What do you, sir, know of that?" she said, to which he replied, "I am the son of Mother Earth and brother to the Feminine Divine. We are one and all, and you, sister Stella, are a goddess. Believe it. Allow it. Be it." He paused to refresh the fire and himself.

"You've had a journey unlike any other," he said, "All who walk this path have their own tales, and I have heard many, yet I have heard none like yours." "I can't imagine you ever will," she laughed and let the words she spoke settle in as they clicked cups and relaxed by the fire.

"Have you been to the Edge of Shadows Inn?" she inquired after a bit. He had never heard of it, though he was aware of Tipping Point and the Banyan Tree. "You walked here across the ancient Banyan. It supports itself eternally and creates bridges to our universal energies. If that is where you stayed the night, you were sleeping in a conduit of celestial resonance."

"Of course I was!" Stella laughed. It made perfect sense. They both looked towards the tree. Its size was so big, the bridge she walked there on was one of many. There were perhaps even infinite bridges as the more she looked, the more she saw, in every direction imaginable—and all seemingly with intention.

When her eyes returned to Daimon, she saw a sliver of gold again. This time, she thought she saw scales. "Did you say you were a dragon?" Stella sheepishly asked. A huge smile took over his face, "Yes! I am a Forest Dragon, from a tribe of wanderers. I am a protector of the trees. It is my role to balance the energy of forest and fire."

Spiraling Up

"That's amazing," she replied, "I hope you don't mind me saying, but in certain light, I see a shimmer across your face, like a gilded cheek. Am I seeing your dragon self?" With a big breath, he puffed up and bellowed, "Oh I hope so! I have never seen my own dragon face, so I do not know what it looks like. I sometimes see red and gold on my body, and I have a searing tongue the color of coal.

"I've also seen fire run beneath my scales, like lava, but it doesn't burn. Because I live in the forests and under the canopy of the trees, I am cooled. My reds become rosy and my golds tarnish with a wash of green. I can feel it cool my fire. I am truly at peace there." His voice wandered off as he thought back to the forests and sipped from his cup.

"I'm honored to have met you. Thank you so much for sharing your story—and your fire," Stella said, raising her glass to him. Acknowledging her sentiment while casually dismissing it, he continued, "Though I honor my dragon lineage, my form varies—sometimes man, sometimes dragon. As a man, I am a Fire Keeper, always ready to welcome a fellow traveler to my camp. I do not have wings so traveling by foot as a human is much easier, and I generally have much more fun with people. Could you imagine joining a dragon at a fireside?" He laughed, then reflectively said, "I think it would be a lonelier life had I only been a dragon."

He raised his glass one more time, "Here's to being who we choose, how we choose, when we choose." "Here, here," Stella cheered in tandem, and with a clink, they sipped and sat back in their chairs for a quiet moment listening to the fire. Crackle, hiss, crackle, pop—the dancing flames and sounds lulled her into a quiet Zen-like mind.

The fire began winding down, motivating her host to cook a little food on the hot rocks before it was out completely. A little bit of bread, some eggs, some fruit. He put a hole in the center of a slice of bread, laid it on a hot flat rock and cracked an egg in the hole. It quickly cooked hard, and he peeled it off the rock. Handing it over, he said proudly, "It's a dragon eye!" As if looking up at her, the yolk became a golden eye of dragon deliciousness, and she enjoyed the first bite as much as each that followed.

After breakfast, he began to break down the fire pit, ready to wander until he found the place to ignite the flame that evening. "Thank you so much for this morning," Stella said, "It was delightful!" Nodding in agreement, he added, "Goddess Stella, you have blessed my morning with the kind of warmth a fire can't offer. Thank you!"

She assisted with putting out the fire safely and realized they would be wandering in different directions. Before they departed, he offered a last bit of guidance: "I can sense you have taken the hard road for a while and have done the work to rise from each fall and learn the lessons revealed, so there may be a detour ahead. Look for the language of light embedded in the boulders as you pass by. If they reveal themselves to you, there may be a new path just beyond them."

"I will look for it!" she replied, smiling as they began to walk their separate ways. After a few paces, she looked back at him, and for the first time, saw his other self. He was looking back at her, waving his claw-like hand, taloned and red. He was large, like she imagined a dinosaur might be, and his large fiery eyes still flickered with the spirit of the man within.

His body was made of colors that symbolized heat, and his face was pure gold. It was all topped by a grinning smile from pointy ear to pointy ear. After a moment, he turned to walk and his tail moved back and forth, covered with scaley armor, yet fluid in its sway. Stella stared with curiosity trying to observe all she could, and when she blinked, she saw the man again. With that, she turned and walked her own path.

Spiraling Up

Sunlight on a Dragons Back

DEEP DIVE DETOUR

From Here to There

As Stella left the field and continued to spiral up the mountain, she noticed the path getting steeper. Looking ahead, she saw she wasn't far from a switchback, nearly a U-turn going up the other direction. As she followed it up, she saw the upwards back and forth continue to narrow without end.

Her feet carried forward as she replayed the places and their lessons, the people, the gifts and the beings. She steeped in the wonderment of it all, realizing she felt understood, connected and content; there was a self-assuredness she couldn't recall having felt before.

As the trail narrowed, she started to think of the footsteps left behind from the base of the mountain to here; from sinking to unsteady to stable and strong, one step after the other, she had evolved.

"I am not the Stella who started this climb," she said, sensing she was a refined version of herself; renewed and recalibrated to her own compass. "I found a sense of direction and inner harmony!" She laughed, knowing it was just the beginning of her symphony. After a bit, she heard the trickle of water and stopped to sip a few handfuls from a small cascade streaming from the side of a rock wall.

A beam of sunlight peaked through a drifting cloud and cast upon the boulder, creating a shimmer to catch her eye. Without hesitation, Stella pulled back a curtain of ivy to reveal a pink crystal embedded in the rock. This must have been what the Fire Dragon Daimon mentioned, for it was certainly calling to her.

Having no idea what it meant, every part of her came alive when she saw it. Much like in the Full Spectrum Stretch, she felt like a snow globe that had just been shaken, and her inner being was moving and active in reaction to an outer force that shook her in the most joyful way. Clearly this moment was meant for her.

An Invitation Sigil

She ran her hand along the art which seemed to be made of rose quartz. She could not imagine how this could be embedded in stone like that, other than by simply believing that it was, so she did.

When ready to take the next step, she followed along the large stone wall as it gently turned into a new path. It kept bending, winding gently until it ended at an earthen wall veiled by tiny blue flowers.

A few steps closer and the flowers flew off the vine. "Butterflies!" she squealed in delight. It was the simplest of joys that filled her cup to overflowing in record time. It was then she realized it wasn't a wall at all and pulled back greenery again to find yet another symbol at the entry of a hidden passage. She immediately knew it was from Serophant, a cryptic *woohoo*!

Serophant Marks the Spot

What did Daimon call this? A detour? "Yes!" she answered herself, "I've been doing the hard work, and now perhaps I am able to find my ascension with less effort." The paw print on the wall, a high-four, felt like validation from her guide for making it there. The detour itself was its own reward. She had found an easier path, and that alone was something to be grateful for.

As she entered, she found the walls lined with images, which created intense waves of energy around her. She was calm, clear and ready, though for what, she still did not know. Deeper into the passage, the environment became cave-like though the light remained bright above her through an open channel that helped to guide her along. Art lined the walls like an ancient gallery; some carved, others painted, and a few were made of inlayed crystals like the first one she encountered.

Recharging Through Love

    She believed the crystal art was in the language of light. She felt cosmic energy emitting from it, a different resonance from the others. Each color was a different stone; red ruby, pink quartz, blue lapis, black shungite. She knew crystals had their own healing properties, symbolism and resonance, and she had no doubt each was chosen to amplify the power of the stones in the message. Someday she hoped to understand it more.

Deep Dive Detour

A Soul's Life Sigil

Stella spent a bit of time absorbing all she could from each piece, in memory, spirit and energy. "I will absorb these images so I may recall them later. I will remember this journey and I will recreate them to learn, recall and expand my connection to this place and all it offers." *Oh, that feels good,* she thought, then she remembered aloud, "RICH! And as if by magic, all paths to help me do so will align to allow the best possible outcomes. RACE! Reality Reset! Woohoo!" Bursting out with laughter, she thrust her hands in the air like she had made a touchdown. "That felt like a big win, Stella!" she said to herself while dancing in place for a moment or two.

A Soul's Happiness Sigil

Overall it was a slow journey in creamy mottled light. She felt relaxed and focused so as not to miss anything. It was as if she was studying artifacts on display in a museum, except she could touch

Spiraling Up

these and examine them closely. It was like the quiet part of a video game where she got to find treasures and linger, so she did.

A New Self Image Sigil

Aside from the sun, a softer light seemed to be coming from the core of large crystal pillars poking out of the earth walls like luxury sconces. The crystals glowed like the blue ones on Falling-Up Hill, only these were purple.

Pulsing tones from brilliant pink to the deep purples of midnight called in the feelings of a loving connection. A synchronistic flow was happening around her between the rhythm of her breathing and the glow. She was enjoying this moment very much, feeling one with the mountain.

Crystals Light the Way

Reminiscent of the chakras, the hues of pinks and purples opened the channels to the best and most meaningful of things. Gentle pinks called in the warmth of love, while a bold fuchsia color lit the fires of her soul in her high heart. Purples rule the crown, the highest peak of our own body and a portal to new connections, energies and wisdoms. She was feeling all of it, in abundance, as evidenced by the tears streaming down her cheeks.

Embracing all the warm fuzzies, feeling love and joy overflowing, she came across an image of a moon in a mosaic of stones and carvings embedded in an alcove. In it, she saw the faces of dear friends and the phases of moons shared; many years, even many lives. Thinking of them made her wonder what her tribe would have to say when she shared the story of this moment.

Moon Sisters Sigil

Further down the way, she saw a smoothed piece of tree root that was curving like a ribbon down the earth wall. Painted upon it in many colors, there appeared to be a totem. Four animals aligned in a column, all of which she recognized: a bull, a dog, a hummingbird and a hawk. Each one spoke to her, and unlike much of the other art, she knew the meaning of this immediately.

Sitting down on the soft mossy floor with her back against the other side of the narrow space, Stella began to speak to herself as a way to integrate the meaning of it fully. "This is my totem pole. Each animal is a touchstone for HOW I connect to myself and the world around me. Every day, I choose to touch upon each, either in action or acknowledgement. I honor and strengthen the connections that help me create my best path.

"The Bull represents the physical self. My physical well-being is the foundation of my stability. I will acknowledge and honor what I DO for this touchstone on any given day, knowing it may change every day, and be okay with it.

"The Dog represents the emotional self. I will acknowledge and honor how I FEEL when my attention is drawn to my emotions. Do I want to feel this way? If not, what can I change to feel differently?

"The Hummingbird represents the intellectual self. I will honor quiet moments, for they are the birth of creation. Action is born in the mind. I will DISCERN what I put the power of my thoughts to.

"The Hawk represents the spiritual self. A messenger from above, a seer and a guide, it reminds me to seek a higher vision, SOAR above the fray and dive deep when called to nourish."

my totem pole

She had no idea how long she sat there receiving that surge of awareness. It was a lot to absorb fully, even though it fit into her consciousness like a missing puzzle piece. It all made perfect sense. It all felt right, like a truth she always knew but had just heard for the first time.

She peeled herself up from the comfort of her seat and continued down the path. "That was like the light at the end of a tunnel," she laughed to herself, as if on cue to the literal light ahead she saw a breath later. Laughing yet again at the kismet of it all, she knew this chapter of her journey was about to break through to not just a space that was open and bright, but also to a self that was as well.

The light ahead was indeed the end of the passage. She hadn't seen anymore art since the totem, and her attention was fixed on the environment around her while her mind spilled through the touchstones and their place in her life.

There were a few steps to climb ahead, boulders leading up and out. On the last step, she reached a hand up to steady herself before landing on a threshold made of slate. When she stood tall and removed her hand, a silhouette of it remained. It was dark gray like a watermark on a lighter gray stone.

As she stared, she saw a fine blue line appear from the center of the palm print. It spiraled outward five times, getting bigger each time yet staying within the size of her palm. At the base of the handprint as if released from the end of the line was a single violet-blue waterlike drip, the same color as the crystal in her crown.

This reminded Stella to reach up to the top of her head and of course, she was still wearing it. It had become one with her and never left her noggin. "Okay," she said "wow," and with that, she knew the new sigil was for claiming this journey as her own. "The spiral is emanating from my core self, allowing who I am to spiral up and out, releasing the essence of life, a droplet of the soul-self that makes me *me*."

Shaking her head affirmatively, feeling as if she was coming back into her own body from a step away, she nodded with lightness as an energetic high-five back to Serophant to close the loop. "Our hands will never be empty," she said, "Thank you."

I Am Here

THE PORTAL
Open Hearts Carry No Baggage

Taking her first step off the landing, she settled on forested soil layered with years of fallen leaves and bark, which felt cushiony below her feet. Each step was like walking on a feathered pillow, very different from the compressed soils and slate she had been on.

Stella saw a path up ahead and wound herself through a series of high-topped trees that were tall and sparse and worn down by the wind, which was quite intense and constant as she left the protection of the rock walls. Neither hungry nor tired, she found a pace that matched her excitement. She knew the summit was ahead and figured something must be waiting for her, and of course, she was right.

The path was like much of what she had passed with flora and fauna everywhere, though the landscape, temperature and air were different, and this was reflected in what flourished. Speaking to herself, she noted, "The parts of me that thrive change in varied environments too. Different catalysts change the evolution of both myself and the environment. It's a full circle interconnected life we live, and the landscape is a beautiful way to remind me of that. Thank you," she said with a grateful nod.

Yeti Peak

Past the sage and tall grasses, and past the naked trees and wind-blustered shrubs, she saw a nook that was pitch black. Then, she heard a rustling. "And now there is a humble mumble?" she queried, looking curiously towards an unseen source of a louder grumble emanating from the shaking brush nearby. She was concerned she was disturbing the peace of another creature, then instantly knew not to worry, for in her body she heard, "Greetings," though nothing was externally audible.

Out from the brush stepped a foot, half her body size, covered in long flowing white hair, or was it fur? It did not matter. Then, a leg followed as a massive hand moved the brush aside, followed by shoulders pushing through and then the torso and another leg, one massive limb at a time until it stood before her.

Three times her size—at least—with ice blue eyes and a humanoid gorilla-like body, the Yeti stood tall, dangling long arms relaxed to the side. Stella stared and for the second time on this journey, she curtsied. Never taking her eyes off the Yeti, she could not hide her awe, so she embraced it by honoring the majesty of the being before her the best way she knew how.

No words were spoken, but there was earnest communication. The humble mumble was like a growl, but it didn't ignite fear. It felt firm, meaningful, intentional and gentle. She did not speak Yeti, but she heard it as if a translator was built into her mind. Words spilled out of the sounds and carried their meaning in a way she could understand.

"I am AlaBastion the Yeti, a being of light and guardian of resilience, and you have come to the Point of Reconciliation. I use my sound waves to destroy and push out the crumbs of what doesn't belong, the bits remaining after all you've accomplished, disintegrating them so they fall like dust freeing your spirit, heart and mind." And with that, AlaBastion's words faded to a rumble again.

Stella felt the surface beneath her vibrate, and then she felt it begin to rise up through her feet. The sensation was centering. She imagined a line through her crown (yes, it was still on) straight through her, down into the soil, like a grounding rod, except in her mind, it was golden. There were waves of energy, sound and vibration ascending the imaginary golden rod and sending rings outward from her core, through her body, her light body and beyond into the infinite. It was clear what was happening, but also completely foreign.

She believed that what she put out into the world flowed infinitely; through her loved ones, her pets and even strangers. Her being mattered, but in this moment she could actually see it. *What you are is what you resonate, our energy bounces off others and is returned altered by theirs and the many other bouncing sources in between. It can get confusing if we aren't clear about what we accept in return as our own.*

The vibrations became a full spectrum experience with sound and color. First, she could hear a hum reminiscent of gently activated crystal healing bowls, a singular resonant tone. Different rings expanding from her core radiated different tones as they moved up and down.

Spiraling Up

She quickly noted there was a connection between the chakras and the tones. Her feet, hands, groin, belly, heart, chest, throat, third eye, crown and then back down all followed in tonal order.

There are many chakras between the ones we know.

As the colors shifted gently, the sounds sang them out in sequence. As they did, the singular tones became harmonic, full and connected. No longer a solo performance, it became a symphony, her symphony.

The colors slowly became brighter and more vibrant. Each hue became stronger along with the tone as it passed through her with the energy field the Yeti embodied and projected.

Stella's legs wobbled, her spine tingled, her pain lessened, her heart pounded and her ears popped! *Open your heart to hear what is needed, both by you and others.*

There were fewer and fewer blips in her radiance, and she began to feel a weightlessness; perhaps it was a lift from the energy around her. She felt a breeze move through her, like an old room whose door was opened and flushed with fresh air for the first time in years. Stagnancy was suddenly gone, and a newness burst through. She heard her own words in a voice once stolen, speaking a story of love for herself, one of inner strength and full awareness, though she was silent in the moment.

With that, the Yeti let out a "ROHHHHR," propelling a visible wavelength as far as she could see. Everything it passed through shuddered, including Stella. She felt it change her. She felt minuscule granules release from hidden crooks within. She felt the last of her emotional burdens disintegrate. The barriers of shame and the *shoulds* and *tried* and *not good enoughs* all fell away into dust. The Yeti was a master illuminator, finding and clearing the last bits of anything she had missed that she did not want to take with her beyond this point.

She took a deep breath and looked directly into AlaBastion's eyes. With a gentle and grateful smile, she reached her hand out and said,

"I. Am. Stella." The Yeti reached a finger out, larger than her hand could wrap around, and chirped a snappy retort almost like a laugh, sending out an "I know." and then patting her on the head. With that, the Yeti turned around and headed back into the bushes, then promptly stopped.

Turning back to her silently, the Yeti pointed and wagged a hand towards the nook, showing her where she would be heading next to conclude her journey. And with that, the Yeti tucked into the brush and was gone.

Before she did anything else, Stella felt a need to physically shift herself. She began to stretch her arms out and up, move her neck in circles, and methodically bend forward towards the ground, stretching everything she could. She moved like never before and she gasped in surprise when she could touch her toes, something that was only a fantasy until this moment.

She felt free of debris and unencumbered; it was an unfathomable feeling. She said thank you again to the long-gone Yeti and followed it with a *Reality Reset*. En route to her next destination, she started to explore where she was.

She was actually at the top of the mountain! With a growing sense of accomplishment, she decided to call it Yeti Peak. The area was mostly surrounded by dense brush, but there was a small trail that ran along the exposed rock walls. It was narrow like a deer path. She hugged a large boulder as she squeezed by to avoid the bristling brush and brambles reaching for her.

Around the bend was a small clearing without trees, but it did have a few shrubs that were low and sparse. The sun was warm on her face, and the sky was a clear gentle blue, the kind she didn't have to squint to enjoy.

In the distance, there were many peaks, many mountains, and an infinite amount of other paths. *Is each mountain another person's journey? Is one mountain many people's journey? Others are on my path too, like the symphony-goers and caravan inhabitants. Perhaps we share more than just a passing moment in time.* Stella knew many people who led very different lives than her own and walked thousands of paths she never traveled.

"To each their own," she said as she became acutely aware that many souls must coexist on shared paths, neighboring mountains and their ranges that extend infinitely. *We are one,* she thought. "Now I'm ready for what's next," she said as she turned back to the little path towards the mysterious passage.

Infinite Paths

When she got closer, it didn't become any clearer. She stood before a dark doorway. Carved into the rock above it were the letters HCCRM. There was no sense of knowing that flooded in upon reading it; it was just there. No signs or feelings caught her attention. She felt neutral. With no driving force to propel her, it was evident the next step would only be taken on her own volition.

Was she ready? Was this the end of the journey? Did she learn all she was supposed to? "Oh Stella, there is no *supposed to*." Catching her old habit, she then paused and caught her new ones. "Calling out my bad habits is not an old habit, which means I am changing. It's the little things that lead to big change."

There really is no end to this journey and she knew it. "I can choose to evolve and grow and shift every day. There are no *have to's* or *should haves*, but there are choices that need to be made. I can feel the yes and no. I can discern the way because it is lit up with signs telling me it's there to take. I need only be open to it, find it and trust it to be real. It's that easy!" she concluded, laughing because it felt like she finally believed it.

Feeling those words deeply in her belly, she added, "May the barriers on my journey guide me to the best outcomes. RICH! As if by magic, let it be so. RACE!" And with that a woosh of energy flowed out of her and the once blackened nook began to shimmer. The doorway shifted and she mumbled a "Reality Reset." In that moment a flash of light expanded from the doorway and she confidently stepped in.

Spiraling Up

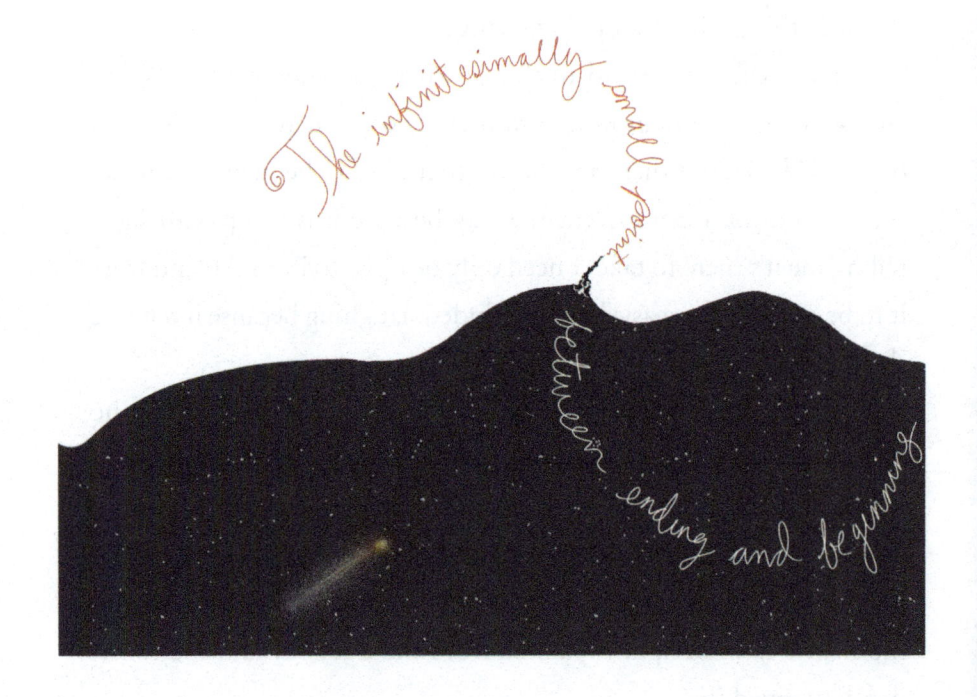

The infinitesimally small point between ending and beginning

EPILOGUE

The Spiral Up

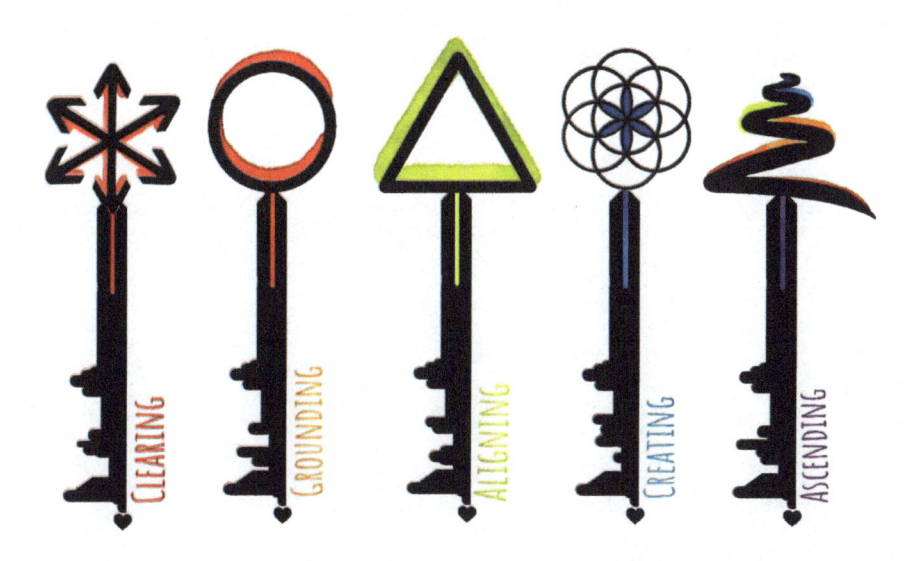

THE END OF THE BEGINNING

Living Your Being

Stella sat at her desk. "I'm home? Yes, I am home." Somehow it did not surprise her to be home any more than it surprised her to be on top of a mountain a moment ago. It was a wild ride. She sat there until she realized she remembered everything, up to the moment she stepped into the light.

Then she sat a while longer. Allowing her mind and body to catch up; she was experiencing a bit of cosmic jet lag and she needed to steady herself in this realm. She focused on her breathing first. Then she grounded herself into the chair by centering her spine, then finding the hum of energy in the room and her place in it. She felt integrated.

She was starting to feel home after just a few moments, recalling the safety and comfort that once came with it, something she hadn't felt there in a long time. As she regained her senses and the space she was in became more relevant, she realized her laptop was on and displaying a new document, one she had no recollection of having written.

Inside the light
I become tethered to source
My heart is high in neon pinks

Spiraling Up

Connecting to the divine
I am mastering human love with my
Heart Coherent Connector Receptor Mechanism

Connect and disconnect
Expand and protect
Love does not suffer
Love created is infinite
You are connected and aligned
The universe is open to boundlessly explore
Use my inner compass to go forward
I am Source in Action Through Love

It was a stream of consciousness. The untitled document was just created, and journaled what she experienced during the one moment she had no memory of. *AHHH* she thought, Heart Coherent Connector Receptor Mechanism, HCCRM—that's what was written over the portal. Her notes continued:

I am greeted by a long line of Ascended Masters
Propelled with gratitude, by love, in harmony with:
Ascended Master Buddha who placed his golden flame
in my heart to reflect his light through love

The End of the Beginning

Ascended Master Isis who cleansed me in her waters
and invites me to return when in need
Ascended Master Kuan Yin protecting and holding boundaries
for the greatest good with love, grace and femininity. She placed
radiant deep pink in my high heart to reflect in Buddha's flame
Ascended Master Tara's Starlight delivers full
spectrum compassion and love
Ascended Master Mother Mary's divine light
will warm my spirit when I cannot
Archangel Michael put down his sword and held
love for me until I could hold it for myself
Gaia, Mother of Earth speaks through nature, listen closely
The Ancients, guiding masters illuminating
the ways of Amber Healing
God said: "I will not call you in to serve my house.
You are free to serve your purpose. We are one."
Find your crystals. They will protect, enlighten,
connect, and simply be beautiful
I am a child of earth, each footstep, grounded and in tune
I am sister to the Moon and a multidimensional traveler
I am a channel for source energy
I know what needs to be known
And share with others what I have learned
ask for guidance when I need it
Manifest the greatest good for self and others
Allow space for others without losing myself
The absence of what is important often
shines the brightest light upon itself

Spiraling Up

Stella read and reread what she had written. A single document typed like a CliffsNotes reference sheet for her to use as a resource at any time. An essential reminder of what she experienced, her gifts, and the resources she has to create the path that she has only just started to walk.

She was noticing more about where she was now and realized she was wearing her usual clothes and was no longer packed with treasures and trinkets. Despite knowing she couldn't possibly have imagined it all, this note was the only tethering "evidence" of her travels. As quickly as she realized that, she knew proof was irrelevant. The experience was within her, the lessons were present and to her it was very real.

She was inspired to do one more thing, something explorers have done throughout time: make a map of new worlds traversed. *That was the first key.* She recalled when Fredrico first introduced the keys to her as part of her spiral up. Thinking about it more, she collected the second key for Serophant's Garden, to learn a deeper connection to her best self. The third key to attune her symphony in harmony was from the Conductor, and the fourth activated her self-expression in meaningful ways with intention.

The last key she recalled was the Answer Key. Like the list at the end of a puzzle book, the answers were within her all along. Her journey was briefly captured on those pages and making it all more accessible to tap into on any given day, *I guess that's why they call it journaling.* It was all a new way to be, and she felt really good thinking she could actually BE it.

She opened a sketching app on her computer and began to draw some lines and squiggles, intending to finish the sketch later. She added a fish, a swirling path, the tree hut and the geode. As she made her marks, she imagined being able to return to this world anytime by simply looking at this map and putting herself there. Would it be the same, frozen in time, or would it evolve as she did? What about the people she met? Did they move along the path too? She supposed she would find out eventually.

Spiral-Up Mountain

Feeling complete in the moment, she stood up and then reached for the ground to check one more thing. She could still touch her toes! A smile stretched across her face to express the satisfaction she felt being able to do that still. She knew immediately it would become a way for her to check in with herself. Validated again that her new state of being was here to stay, Stella began to wander around her home as if returning from a vacation.

Spiraling Up

She was finding everything in its place. Plants were watered and food was fresh, so she knew she wasn't gone long. All seemed as it was until she opened the front door and found the little box of bark, the gift she never opened on the mountain. Her heart lit up as she reached for it. Looking around, she felt like she was being watched but could not see the observer. "Thank you," she said, beaming a bright smile and holding the box to her chest.

When she sat back down, she was excited to finally open it. She explored the puzzle sides as she had before, only this time she saw it differently. When she lifted the lid, the box sides fell open, revealing three other gifts from her journey, each of which were bigger than the box! Laughing to herself, she reached for the crown, which was sitting on top of the other contents, upright and ready to place on her head, so she promptly did.

The lessons learned while wearing it became part of it and when placed on her head, her third eye opened, and as if filed in cosmic filing cabinets, what she needed at any given moment she knew she could recall at will; and she wouldn't have to wear the crown to do it. It was then that she understood this was the Generator Key Fredrico spoke of. The key was the crown. Foresight, reflection and clear perception—that was the way to generate her possibilities. *If I can see it, I can be it.* She took the crown off and gave it a place of honor nearby. She felt recharged.

Already floating on her cloud, she continued to explore the box. She was excited to find the Qubes, wrapped with a little tag that said *I am Source in Action Through Love*, repeating what she typed a bit ago. "Play is Joy is Love is Qubes," she said out loud with a grin, reiterating Serophant's words.

Lastly, patiently waiting to be found in a soft collection of moss was LaLu Narock, which elicited a delightful sound of glee from Stella that was answered back with a brilliant white light from within the rock. It was all real enough for her and it was too amazing not to share with the world! Yet she hesitated, it was all so strange. She wasn't sure folks would understand, though some of them might.

Then she thought they might belittle her or dismiss it all as entirely foolish. "It's still a YES for me," she decided then and there, "The truth is sometimes ridiculous. If there are many people on my mountain traveling a similar journey they will understand my story, and I believe it can help them with theirs. If someone doesn't understand, then my story wasn't meant for them…and that's okay!" Then she celebrated that new confidence with a little dance.

Sitting down in front of her computer again, she started to wonder what else she might find in this world that connected her to the discoveries she had made. *If the gifts were brought here, there must be other bridges and portals.* Was something connecting the people too? To find out, she started with the easiest place: the internet.

Searches for names of people did not match. Dirt had a million results, but they were not the man. It was comical the random things that did come up, though perhaps not random at all. *If I don't ask, the answers are much harder to find, although asking questions online usually means far more answers than I can handle.* She laughed, knowing that searching through the wisdoms of the universe had much more precise results.

She did follow a few links that piqued her curiosity more than others. Internal nudges guided her click after click, and they began to reveal something unexpected: these people existed. Stella found it truly fantastical that her mystical woo-woo world may have been in her real world all along. She was inspired.

Even more fascinating, tapping into her logical left-brain self, she discovered a science-based study about how the resonance of our heart can change the world by sending out a particular wavelength. *HCCRM* came flooding into her thoughts. "Amazing!" she hollered out, "I can't wait to learn more…later."

Stella had to put a pin in her exploration for bit. Her grumbly tummy informed her it was essential she refresh and feed herself. She was motivated to find more real-world connections and see if there was a new community out there waiting for her to be a part of it, but it needed to wait. That was a rabbit hole of internet searches that she imagined could take a lifetime.

She shifted gears and went about her rituals of care for herself. Now in her home, she appreciated that she was no longer in the elements, though she noticed an absence of the living greens and colors. She decided she would bring those missing pieces in.

Her shower held no comparison to a whirling pool of crystals, but it was enough. It was hot and soothing and it felt just right. She decided her thoughts would be the gems she bathed with and she let them cascade with the water. The ease of her home comforts came to mind, and though she hadn't thought about it much before, she now held gratitude for all they provided. At last, Stella FELT home.

Now in the kitchen, she began to collect the ingredients for a warming pot of Troll food. Veggies, herbs, proteins and broth were simmering in no time. She channeled the love FannySi shared when serving her that amazing meal as it seemed to be the most important ingredient of all.

Sitting down to enjoy a hearty bowl she would have been proud to serve to her new friend, she paid a compliment to the chef with a hearty "YUM!" While refueling her body, she considered how to process all she learned from the last few days; if it had been days, she really had no idea. She felt a pull to do something, yet there was no clarity as to what. Then she recalled the advice a dear friend quietly whispered when tragedy hit: *Write it all down.*

Lost in the despair of grief, the advice became a lifeline, a way to log the tiny miracles and moments that would make or break her day. Writing became an act of rebellion against the dead. SHE LIVED. Nearly lost moments, insignificant and fleeting, were captured by her words and they became significant; just as her portal pages had done today.

Lifetimes are merely an entry in her soul's journal; but what she had just gone through—that was worthy of a whole book in this life. It was suddenly paramount that she record her ascension up Spiral-Up Mountain, lest it be lost in the haze of a mere mortal's mind.

After eating she returned to the computer with her mind fresh and focused. She wanted to compose her thoughts as if they were the voicings of a symphony in the key of Stella, harmonizing her fantastical adventures with the lessons she learned on her journey up.

Content with a full belly and a comfortable chair, she rested her hands on the keyboard. Knowing that what she had experienced mattered, she started to type.

Once upon a time...

ABOUT THE AUTHOR

In 2017 life came to a screeching halt upon the suicidal death of my husband. Everything I knew, dreamt and imagined suddenly ceased to exist. I had a desperate need to secure my home and cuddle my pets. Grief stripped me bare leaving only a tiny bit of light in my belly and all I could do was crawl into an imaginary hole and protect it.

Plunged into a canyon of despair, I felt like I was at the base of a tall mountain, hiding. Sometimes I would peek out of the cliffside cavern to remind myself how far I'd fallen, or perhaps feel a breeze on my face, maybe hear the birds chirp. I was physically, emotionally and spiritually hobbled.

Grief robbed me of my ability to read, drive, think, plan, taste; yes, I lost my taste buds too. I was a chef at the time, making it all the more traumatic. We owned a small-town cafe and suddenly I was unable to lead, follow or even sustain eye contact. I simply shut down. It wasn't long after that I realized I had no idea what was to become of me, but I knew I would be okay.

As a small child I believed I was destined for good things, though I knew not what they were. It is a deeply held belief that has gotten me through the darkest of experiences; I knew those places were not where I was going to stay. I also believed there was something I needed to learn from these moments in order to get to the good stuff. Not one to repeat difficult things, I learned to reflect and find the wisdom.

Spiraling Up

After his death, I had to go back to basics: believe I would be okay and allow that to be enough.

A life-altering shift started with a yes. That was it. Does it feel okay? Yes? Then okay, let's see what happens. Usually something tickled or tingled or grumbled or thumped in my body and I would follow the yes or no dutifully as it required very little energy or thought, and I could muster neither. It was a simple practice that changed my life.

Once struggling to survive, I am now able to thrive. This book could not exist if not for the yes's that followed that trauma and grief. New people at a vulnerable time became catalysts for a healing journey that connected me to multidimensional portals, spiritually healing wisdoms and galactic travel. They connected me to me. All of this has altered my physical, emotional and spiritual well-being for lives to come and somehow even lives passed.

This book represents my spiral up; from the dark caverns to the sun-soaked peak. I had my instincts and was learning to discern the guidance of others. The choices, however, were my own and they led me up slowly, intentionally and with abundant gratitude.

When I had enough, I said so. When I needed help, I reached out. When I needed a hug, I found one; thankful to have a loving tribe around me to respond. The stories and drawings shared are from my experiences that have come together in the style of old tales told to me by my grandmother. Despite living it, I was often surprised at what fell onto the page as I wrote.

We each have our own journey. Yours will be distinctly you; in fact, that's the point. Find yourself. These pieces of myself came together over many years and then fell into place all at once, right where they belong. This book is a finished puzzle offering you a new world to peer into, one even I hadn't seen until now. For the first time in my journey as an author, I am standing at the top of my mountain, achieving milestones and creating my vision for living my being, part of which is writing this for you.

Thank you for sharing in this moment with me. May it open doorways for your own adventures within.

Many Blessings,
Terra

Spiraling Up

ACKNOWLEDGMENTS

I have accomplished little alone and am blessed and honored to have connected to many wonderful people and places. Those whose impact are on these pages include but most definitely are not limited to:

Lyna, my mom and first love

My Zippity-Do-Da Dad Tory

Cheryl, Diane, Fanny, Forest, Ginger, Isabella,
Jen, Jean, Jenny Jo, Judi
Lya, Keenan, Maria, Macaya, Meghan, Randell,
Stacy, Suzanne, Tom, Tony and Tracy

The twinkle of my Great-Aunt Stella

The open minds and hearts of the generations before me…and after

Energy workers around the world enlightening,
uplifting and healing others

Feroshia & Coach Training World,
Brett & Self-Publishing School and
Sandra, my wonderful editor

JK, from beginning to end

Thank You.

REALITY CHECK

These are but a few of the extraordinary people
and places that exist beyond the story, a story that could not
exist without them. If they resonate with you, reach out.

My experiences are my own and in no way
suggest yours will be similar.

Stella aka Terra Nicolle @ www.AscendingLogic.com

Lady JuJu aka Jenny Clairvoyant @ www.JennyClairvoyant.com

MacA AyA aka Macaya Miracle @
www.MacayaMiracle.beingjoy123.com

Madam AuraCull V z tor aka Maria @ 1-360-809-3358

HCCRM - Randelle @ www.EvolutionaryGuidance.com

Heart Math - Mind Body Connection @ www.HeartMath.com

A bridge to many places on the path - The Human and
Fairy Relations Congress @ www.FairyCongress.com

Made in the USA
Monee, IL
08 June 2024